TREETOPS

The Family 🦋

Mary Phipps m. Thomas Watson

Thomas Watson (1854–1934) m. Elizabeth Seaver Kimball (1860–1945)

Thomas (1883–1901)   Ralph (1884–1903)

Elizabeth (1914–1972)   Jane (1915–   )   Thomas (1916–   )
m. Walter Thompson   m. Robert Mellors   m. Elizabeth Austin

Helen   Alice   Thomas
John   Robert   Charles
          William   Sally
          John

Stephen (1911–   )   Frederick (1913–1981)
m. Ethel Lang

Stephen
Dudley
Hannah
Benjamin

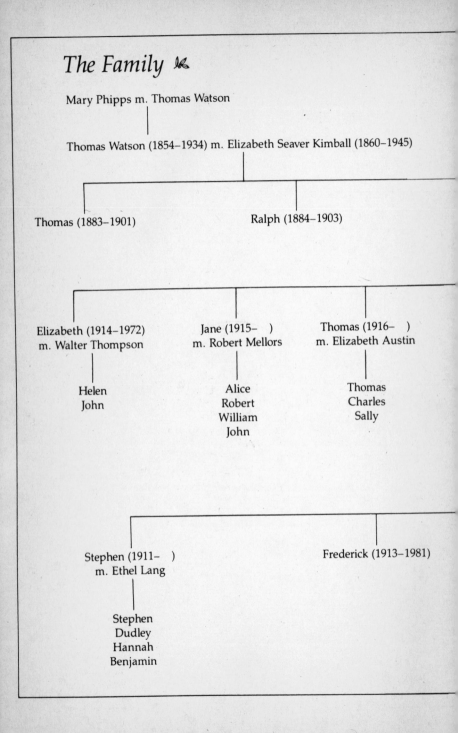

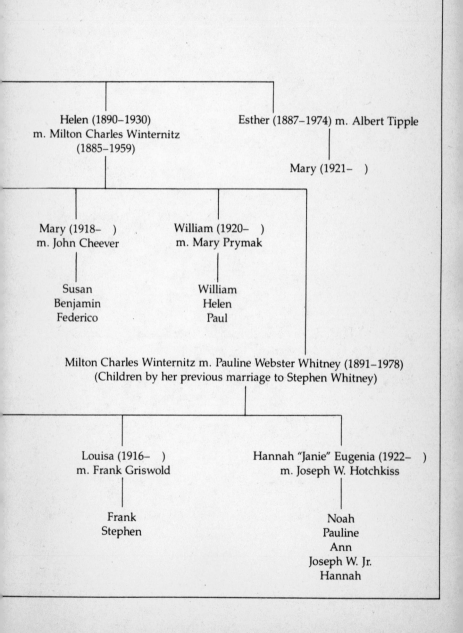

Helen (1890–1930)
m. Milton Charles Winternitz
(1885–1959)

Esther (1887–1974) m. Albert Tipple

Mary (1921–)

Mary (1918–)
m. John Cheever

Susan
Benjamin
Federico

William (1920–)
m. Mary Prymak

William
Helen
Paul

Milton Charles Winternitz m. Pauline Webster Whitney (1891–1978)
(Children by her previous marriage to Stephen Whitney)

Louisa (1916–)
m. Frank Griswold

Frank
Stephen

Hannah "Janie" Eugenia (1922–)
m. Joseph W. Hotchkiss

Noah
Pauline
Ann
Joseph W. Jr.
Hannah

Mary Winternitz Cheever at Treetops, 1940

TREETOPS

A Family Memoir

SUSAN CHEEVER

BANTAM BOOKS
New York   Toronto   London   Sydney   Auckland

Photo insert credits: Insert One, page 1, photo of Thomas and
Elizabeth Watson—AT&T Photographic Archives; page 4, portrait of
Dr. Milton Charles Winternitz by Deane Keller.
No credits required for other photos.

TREETOPS

A Bantam Book

PRINTING HISTORY

Bantam hardcover edition published April 1991
Bantam trade paperback edition / March 1992

Designed by Kathryn Parise.

Library of Congress Catalog Card Number: 90-48251.

For information address: Bantam Books.

ISBN 0-553-35132-X

Published simultaneously in the United States and Canada

Bantam Books are published by Bantam Books, a division of Bantam
Doubleday Dell Publishing Group, Inc. Its trademark, consisting of the
words "Bantam Books" and the portrayal of a rooster, is Registered in
U.S. Patent and Trademark Office and in other countries. Marca Regi-
strada. Bantam Books, 666 Fifth Avenue, New York, New York 10103.

PRINTED IN THE UNITED STATES OF AMERICA

RRH   0 9 8 7 6 5 4 3 2 1

FOR MY WONDERFUL DAUGHTER,
SARAH

That late in the season, the light went quickly. It was sunny one minute and dark the next. Macabit and its mountain range were canted against the afterglow, and for a while it seemed unimaginable that anything could lie beyond the mountains, that this was not the end of the world. The wall of pure and brassy light seemed to beat up from infinity. Then the stars came out, the earth rumbled downward, the illusion of an abyss was lost. [She] looked around her, and the time and the place seemed strangely important. This is not an imitation, she thought, this is not the product of custom, this is the unique place, the unique air, where my children have spent the best of themselves.

—John Cheever, from
"The Day the Pig Fell into the Well"

INTRODUCTION

In 1984 when I finished writing *Home Before Dark*, a book about my father, I thought I had written my family history. In the years since then, as I have raised my own children and started to tell them about their family's past, I began to see that I had told only half the story—my father's story. The myths he created about himself were part of a larger family legacy: a history passed on and embroidered to serve its members.

This book is about family myths: what they reveal and what they hide. It is about three generations of my mother's family and the way their myths were created. It is about the men who made the family famous and the women who lived in their shadows. And as much as anything, this book is about the place where all the myths began: Treetops, a cluster of white cottages on a New Hampshire hillside where my great-grandfather Watson and his daughter and son-in-law built the rustic camp which is still the family summer place four generations later.

◆

We have always been, we tell each other, a family of eccentric and extraordinary men: the oddball genius, my great-grandfather Thomas Augustus Watson; my grandfather, a Jewish Socrates at Yale; my father, an inspired and celebrated writer. The women in my family don't tell many stories about themselves. In a family of storytellers and mythmakers they have always been characters, not creators of characters.

My mother is a talented poet, artist and writer, but she has never had the satisfaction or the responsibility of financially providing for herself and her family by working. She is one of a lost generation of women, women who were isolated between the historic changes of the Depression and World War II and the frantic pace of our society's changing values in the last thirty years. They were supported by men as wives and mothers during the years when their world placed less and less value on being a wife or a mother. The generation before them sanctified motherhood. The generation after them went to work. They were housewives in the decades when "housewife" became a dirty word.

Almost every summer, all her life, my mother has gone to Treetops. She learned to swim in the transparent water of Newfound Lake at the bottom of the hill. She brought her school friends from the Foote School in New Haven there, and later her classmates from Sarah Lawrence. It was where she learned to love and hate, keeping her balance in the family quicksand which included her father, her stepmother, her four brothers and sisters and her four Whitney half brothers and sisters. Her young fiancé, a promising twenty-seven-year-old writer named John Cheever, went to court her there the year after she graduated from college. She spent summers at Treetops when her children were babies, and she has seen her granddaughter christened there.

Time is distorted at Treetops. There's little distinction between the past, the recent past, and the present—except that the present is less vivid. Seven years ago my cousin the Reverend Frank Griswold said the baptismal service for my infant daughter on the oval lawn that is the center of Treetops. My daughter is a second-grader now, Frank is the bishop of Chicago. We all stood above the orchard in the sun, and he blessed her with water from Newfound Lake. My own father had been dead just a few months then, and I could feel him standing there, the way he used to, in baggy shorts and a frayed Brooks shirt, squinting down toward the lake to see if the water was too rough for canoeing. He looked as if he wasn't quite used to the sunlight.

Treetops in its heyday in the 1940s and 1950s was run like an English country house by my grandfather and my step-grandmother, his second wife, Polly Whitney. Polly was my best friend at Treetops when I was growing up. She and my grandfather lived on the downhill side of the orchard in the Stone House, a larger house which had been built for my mother's mother, my grandfather's first wife, Helen Watson. I would play on the gleaming floor of the Stone House with a pack of cards from Polly's large collection—my favorite were royal blue with her monogram in gold—while she and my father shook dice over the backgammon board in front of the fireplace and drank martinis from a shaker. First they would have what they called their preprandial libation. Then we would all walk up the hill to the dining porch, where my grandfather held court from the head of the table, and they would have their drinks with lunch. Then, after lunch, they would have their postprandial libation, and so on. By dinnertime they were in a very good mood.

Everyone dressed for dinner, and there were cocktails at the Stone House at six fifteen. At six forty-five, the cook rang a brass bell from the kitchen porch and they all walked up the hill as well as they could. If I was down at the Stone House, my grandfather, Dr. Milton Charles Winternitz, would give me a ride in the rumble seat of his shiny black Buick convertible. I called him Gram. Everyone else called him Winter. Each of Winter and Polly's nine children and stepchildren would be invited to Treetops for a month during the summer. The place had a glamour and luxury beyond what they had achieved in their own lives. There were lots of servants, a good cook, and a guest list that included Winter's famous colleagues from Yale, his friends like University of Chicago president Robert Hutchins, Dr. Harvey Cushing, Polly's friends from society, and anyone else who dropped in—visitors as diverse as Gypsy Rose Lee and the son of the local grocer.

The Winternitz "children," my mother and her four siblings, were in their twenties and thirties with children and households of their own, but their emotional drama in relation to their father and stepmother and their half brothers and sisters continued undiminished as if they were still kids. Those out of favor were usually asked to stay in an uncomfortable cottage like Spruce, a dark apartment over the garage, and were also pointedly excluded from the jolly goings-on during cocktail hour at the Stone House. They were left to drink their own whiskey out of the toothbrush glasses in their cottages until they heard the dinner bell and the sounds of merriment from the more favored children as they made their way up the hill. Then they would go to dinner and smile and chat as if nothing could be more pleasant.

This book is about Treetops and the family who came of age there, gathering together each summer on a remote New Hampshire hill to tell their stories: the stories that Tom Watson told his grandchildren and the ones he wrote for posterity— one of which has become part of American history; the stories my grandfather told as the father of nine children and the dean of medicine at Yale; and my father's stories, not only the nursery stories he told me starring a rabbit named Pauline who snacked on the flower beds at the Stone House, but also the fabulous stories he wove using the threads of our lives at Treetops.

Treetops
August 1989

PART ONE

ONE

TREETOPS WAS BUILT out of my great-grandfather Tom Watson's dreams. Born grit poor in a Salem, Massachusetts livery stable, Watson got rich and famous in the 1870s, when he and his friend Alexander Graham Bell invented and developed the telephone. Watson was an inspired technician, a clever storyteller, a driven adventurer, and a man who lost a lot of money banking on the innate goodness of human nature. He spent the bulk of his Bell millions building a shipyard which employed most of eastern Massachusetts during the depression of the 1890s—he joked that it would have been cheaper to pension off every able-bodied man in the state. His unorthodox management methods—Watson liked to bid on huge navy battleships his Fore River shipyard wasn't equipped to build, figuring that if he won the bid he'd expand—sent the shipyard's treasurer into a sanatorium with a nervous breakdown, but Watson managed to produce five of the cruisers and battleships in President Theodore Roosevelt's navy, and two of his ships went around the world with the proud Great White Fleet. When the ship-yard's creditors finally foreclosed, Watson had saved enough to live on if he supplemented his income with writing and lectures, and to buy the fifty acres on a hillside in New Hampshire which is still the geographical center of his family.

Watson believed that the rich owed the poor. With his friend Edward Bellamy, the American writer and socialist, he founded the Nationalist political party. He also panned for gold in Alaska, studied classical music, committed most of Shakespeare's plays to memory, and became a geologist who had a fossil—Watsonella—named after him. In his fifties, Watson joined Frank Benson's traveling company of Shakespearean players and toured the small towns of England. Fully costumed in armor or togas, he proclaimed his lines—"Ave Brutus!" was one—from the ramshackle stages at Bath, Birmingham, and Liverpool.

In my family, conventional success at formal education has always been taken as a sign of a dull, law-abiding nature. My father was expelled from school at seventeen and wrote his first story about it. My grandfather Milton Charles Winternitz graduated at fifteen. Watson quit school in Salem when he was fourteen. By the time his classmates were getting their degrees, he was chumming around with Queen Victoria and Kaiser Wilhelm and trying to decide how to invest his personal fortune. He believed in reincarnation of the soul after death, the curative powers of daydreaming, and taxing the rich—and he loved a good story. At Treetops he enthralled his grandchildren with tailor-made tall tales about a boy named Tom who invented a car that ran on milk—and that made ice cream, a boy named Bill who was taught to swim in the lake by a talking fish, and a girl named Mary who discovered underground tunnels which enabled her to chat with the carrots and potatoes whose tops were growing in the vegetable garden. Watson's most skillful and enduring story is the one he made up about the first words spoken over the telephone wires, on the evening of March 10, 1876, in the attic rooms Bell rented in Boston.

According to Watson, writing in his 1926 autobiography, *Exploring Life*, the historic words were Alexander Graham Bell's shout for help after he knocked over a beaker of battery acid. Bell was always clumsy. "Mr. Watson, come here, I want you!" he called in pain, and Watson, standing in the next room, heard the words transmitted through the wire. Since then, this story of the birth of the telephone has been repeated in thousands of biographies, history textbooks, and educational films, and even in a movie, *The Story of Alexander Graham Bell*, starring Don Ameche.

The fact that it didn't happen this way has not diminished the story's dramatic impact.

There was no accident, there was no spilled battery acid. "The first recorded message was commonplace," Watson complained in a letter soon after the event. "There was little of dramatic interest in the occasion," he wrote to another correspondent. There is no reference to the accident with acid in any log or letter of Bell's or in Watson's log for the day.

It wasn't until Watson sat down to remember this historic moment in his autobiography, fifty years after the fact, that the spilled acid was invented. Watson was an old man, and the past had become dim and malleable. Bell was dead and couldn't contradict him. Watson was living in retirement in a fisherman's cottage on the Florida beach, and his impulse to tell a good story finally became irresistible.

"I was astonished to hear Bell's voice coming from [the receiving telephone] distinctly saying, 'Mr. Watson, come here, I want you!'" Watson wrote in *Exploring Life*. "He had no receiving telephone at his end of the wire so I couldn't answer him, but as the tone of his voice indicated that he needed help, I rushed down the hall to his room and found he had upset the acid of a battery over his clothes. He forgot the accident in his joy over the success of the new transmitter when I told him how plainly I had heard his words, and his joy was increased when he went to the other end of the wire and heard how distinctly my voice came through."

Like all inspired storytellers, Watson altered the facts just slightly, drawing what *should* have happened out of what did happen. In remembering my father's stories about his life—decades after Watson's—I often noticed that this was exactly what he did. If a moment in his career was triumphant, like the moment when an editor bought his first novel, my father would fashion a triumphant moment out of the mundane available facts. A rowboat would become a yacht, a chance meeting at a cocktail party would become a Stanley-meets-Livingstone encounter on a beach after a thrilling approach down the reach of Nantucket Harbor. Of course none of us *expected* accuracy from my father. He made his living by making up stories. So it was thrilling to discover that the so-called scientific side of my family had been doing the same thing all along, starting with Great-grandfather Watson.

Perhaps, as he wrote about the invention of the telephone,

Watson remembered a previous incident with acid and spliced the two together. Maybe he had heard about someone else having an accident with spilled acid. Using the techniques of storytelling as skillfully as a novelist, he wrote such a compelling account of that evening in 1876 that the spilled battery acid has become part of American history.

By the time the Wit and Wisdom of Great Men is passed on, they are usually bearded, somber-looking stiffs. Their pale faces stare out at us lesser mortals from postage stamps, portraits, and official histories. Watson and Bell are no exception; even in the pictures of them as young men, they are unsmiling and sober-sided, clearly mindful of the important fate which destiny holds in store for them. But in 1874 when Watson, a stable boy turned electrical engineer, met Bell, a Scot who made a living tutoring deaf children with a system called Visible Speech, at Charles Williams' grimy machine shop on Court Street in Boston, they were not elder statesmen. They were a couple of kids with a few inspired ideas embarking on a mission impossible—the invention of a method for carrying a sound-shaped current through electrical wires which would carry the human voice.

Williams' was one of a few crude machine shops in the country which manufactured electrical equipment—telegraph parts, fire alarms, electric call bells and other gadgets. In the gas-light age, electricity was a commodity reserved for the very rich or the very modern. The shop was on the third floor and attic of a dusty old building on Court Street. Belts and pulleys whirred overhead as the men worked with their hammers, chisels and lathes, stepping over piles of castings and steel rods to get to their benches against the greasy walls. Williams' shop

was an informal center for local inventors, those kinky vision-
aries who needed to see their ideas transformed into wire,
metal and cable—often overnight. Thomas Edison had worked
at Williams' shop, and Moses Farmer had invented the electric
fire alarm there. But most of the drawings being worked on in
the shop were for contraptions like corn-husk-fueled engines
and exploding submarine mines.

Watson was twenty-one and Bell was twenty-seven when they
met at Williams'. Watson worked all day at the shop on their
ideas and then the two of them stayed up most of the night
tinkering and talking. When something went well they burst
into a howling, stomping war dance that almost got them
evicted from their cheap, boardinghouse rooms. "Watson! I believe we are on the verge of a great discovery!" Bell would intone
before each experiment. They were always broke, and Bell's
financial backers, Thomas Sanders and Gardiner Hubbard,
urged him to give up the idea of the telephone and work on
something more practical.

It was the electricity generated by their friendship that kept
Bell and Watson working against the odds. Watson was an
elegant natural technician from a crude background. Bell was a
thinker and a gentleman who could never make the machinery
keep up with his ideas. Watson showed Bell how to make wire,
metal, and wood into something that worked. Bell introduced
Watson to classical music and gentlemanly manners; he taught
him to stop swearing and to eat with a fork.

The late nineteenth century in Boston was a fertile time for
dreams. The city had named itself the "Athens of America."
Longfellow was teaching at Harvard, and Oliver Wendell
Holmes held forth at the law school. Electric trolleys and trains

provided fast, clean transportation. The clear water of the harbor was crowded with yachts, packets, and the great schooners and sailing ships which carried on a rich trade with the Orient, taking raw cotton, tobacco, lumber, and wool, and returning with their holds packed with Huk-wa tea, coffee, and silks, jammed in with blue and white Canton china for ballast.

The Boston Common was transformed from a mucky cow pasture into a lush labyrinth of paths and trees with a bandstand. The festering waters of Back Bay had been filled in and the new land laid out in broad boulevards where Bostonians built spacious mansions designed by Richardson, Olmstead, and White. Fannie Farmer was writing the book which would introduce recipes with precise measurements and make a science out of the art of cooking. Elias Howe had just invented the sewing machine. An English visitor named Charles Dickens was living at the elegant Tremont Hotel writing his book about America, and Ralph Waldo Emerson's essays appeared regularly in one of the new magazines—*The Atlantic Monthly*.

There were nine daily newspapers in Boston. The town buzzed with prosperity, from the Italianate palaces built by textile and railroad barons along Commonwealth Avenue to the thriving merchants' shops in Scollay Square where the "Old Howard" was still a respectable playhouse. In 1881 the Boston Symphony was established and George Henschel conducted the second symphony of his friend Johannes Brahms in the new Symphony Hall. Half the audience walked out, afterwards perversely referring to themselves as Boston Brahmins.

The men and women who had hacked this glorious city out of the savage American wilderness in a little more than a hundred years saw no limits to progress in the future. Anything

seemed possible. All problems could be solved by human inge-
nuity and industry. The men who would solve many of them—
the inventors—were raffish prophets whose strange ideas
might sound crazy, but occasionally yielded great fame and an
instant fortune. They were the rock stars of the nineteenth
century.

Even the metaphysical world was not immune to the advanc-
ing frontiers of human understanding. The age of inventors
was also the age of spiritualists. Séances were common enter-
tainment. Watson and his neighbors sat around a table while
their friend George Phillips reached underneath with chalk
and a slate and had his hand "taken" by spirits. A New Hampshire healer named Mrs. Mary Baker Glover, soon to marry Asa
Eddy, announced that she had conquered disease through
faith, and thousands of people crowded into her Christian
Science classes. Madame Blavatsky had just founded Theoso-
phy, a popular combination of eastern religions, and over in
Cambridge the writer William James promised his Yoga teacher
that he would try fasting and deep breathing.

Watson saw his friends "seized" by the spirits of the dead,
jerking their arms and legs convulsively and rolling their eyes.
However, the greatest spiritual influence of his childhood was
his parents' enrolling him in the local Baptist Church and Sunday School—it turned him against organized religion for life.

The greatest discoveries often happen by accident. It's as if
these things are waiting to reveal themselves—waiting until
someone is smart enough to notice what in retrospect seems
obvious. The telephone was no exception. On a steamy afternoon in 1875, when the air was like glue and Watson's fingers
stuck to every surface he touched, he impatiently screwed

down a vibrating reed so tightly that it made an electrical connection. Listening in the next room, Bell heard, not the sound of the reed, but the sound of his assistant plucking the reed. Because he had spent years studying electricity and the nature of sound, Bell knew the meaning of that tiny ping. A sound-shaped current had been carried through the wires. Bell and Watson spent the evening sketching what they thought would be the first working telephone. Watson memorized the sketch on the midnight train home to Salem. At dawn he was on his way back to Boston and his workbench at Williams' shop.

At the end of that day, when the last worker at the shop had gone home, Bell ran upstairs to the attic while Watson attached the telephone to the wires.

"Hoy!" Bell shouted into the mouthpiece. "Hoy! Watson." (All his life Bell insisted that "Hoy" or "Ahoy" was the proper salutation for beginning a telephone conversation. He was appalled by the public insistence on using the pallid "Hello.") Watson could hear Bell's voice, but it sounded like an engine turning over. He couldn't make out the words. During the next weeks, Watson desperately tried to improve the primitive mechanism.

By January of 1876, both men knew that others were at work on a similar invention. For secrecy, Bell rented two rooms on Exeter Place, a few blocks from Williams' shop, furnishing one room as a bedroom and the other as a laboratory. The two friends were on a roll. Watson would work at his bench in the shop all day and then carry his newest machine over to Exeter Place for a night of experimentation and modification. Sometimes he got a few hours of sleep at Bell's before going back to work.

Bell's patent application for the telephone was filed by Gardiner Hubbard in Washington, D.C., that February 14, just a few hours ahead of a similar patent filed by Elisha Gray, a Western Electric Company inventor who had not yet been able to get his wires to transmit sound. Bell was a lucid writer. His first patent described the machine he and Watson were working on so well that it withstood the hundreds of lawsuits brought against the Bell company over the next decade by other inventors who wanted to claim a share of the telephone's enormous profits.

Then on the evening of March 10, Watson carried another transmitter from Williams' shop over to the attic on Exeter Place. This time he had refined the vibrating drumhead which received the sound of the voice and had built the first speaking tube mouthpiece. Heart pounding, he attached the wires. "Watson!" Bell proclaimed, as usual. "I believe we are on the verge of a great discovery!" This time they were. Watson hadn't even settled down to listen when Bell's voice came clearly through the wires. So history was made, and fifty years later Watson transformed history into legend.

All the men in my family have benefited from having a short attention span. Watson was easily bored. By 1881, five years after the first words were spoken through the telephone wires, he wrote Gardiner Hubbard asking for a leave from his job at Bell—at that point a company worth more than $25 million. The list of subjects he wanted to study included rocks, music, and languages. "Such a prospective feast," he wrote, "made the telephone business seem like the rind of yesterday's fruit."

In June 1881 he took off for a year in Europe on the Cunard Line's *Batavia*, bound for Liverpool and points south.

Europe disappointed Watson. In spite of a grand reception in British and European high society, he was homesick for New England and lonely traveling by himself. When he got home, the family story goes, he confided his feelings to his friend Bell over dinner at Kimball's Inn in Cohasset just southeast of Boston.

"It's about time you got married," Bell said, as they tucked into Kimball's shore dinner—huge portions of steamers, fresh oysters, and lobster trapped off the Cohasset ledges. Peter Kimball, the inn's proprietor, was also an inventor of sorts—in his own kitchen he had discovered that a potato, sliced paper-thin and fried in deep fat, made a delicious, crunchy side dish. Heaps of these chips, hot from the pan, were served with his seafood. Kimball's was a family place. Mrs. Kimball was the chef, and the children worked in the dining room, while Peter Kimball circulated from table to table making sure his guests were happy and well fed.

"Perhaps you're right," Watson said, on their second bottle of wine. But, he complained, he didn't know any available young unmarried women.

In the years since Watson and Bell had worked together at Exeter Place, Bell had fallen in love with Gardiner Hubbard's deaf daughter, Mabel. After a rocky courtship—the Hubbards approved of Bell as a teacher but not as a suitor—the two had married and were very happy. Anyway, Watson gallantly wound up, there would never be another woman as sweet or as beautiful as Mabel Hubbard Bell.

"Well," said Bell in a burst of practicality, as their plates were efficiently cleared and more steaming food was placed in front of them. "How about this nice young waitress?"

So it was that Tom Watson married the innkeeper Peter Kimball's daughter Elizabeth in the summer of 1882, and settled on a farm on the Fore River in East Braintree near Cohasset. Tom and Elizabeth Watson had two sons and two daughters, whom she raised while her husband pursued his various enthusiasms—politics, shipbuilding, music, geology, the theater. Her two sons died of childhood illnesses: one of consumption and one of diabetes. It was the Watsons' daughter Helen, her father's favorite, who would break with tradition by going to college and medical school and start the dynasty that had always been her father's dream.

TWO

TOM WATSON WAS not pleased when his daughter Helen insisted on going to college. He was upset when she announced that she was going on from Wellesley to Johns Hopkins to get a medical degree, although she was driven to become a doctor because of her brothers' deaths. He was horrified when she fell in love with her pathology professor, a brash Baltimore boy who had worked his way through school by selling penny insurance door to door. Dr. Milton Charles Winternitz—everyone called him Winter—was already a controversial star in the small world of medical academia. A Jew in a Protestant profession, he was a short man with a tyrannical manner, an intense charm that could make you feel that you were the only person in the world—and a raging temper that could make you wish you weren't.

Helen Watson—genteel, beautiful, and smart—was the girl of his dreams. When Winter wanted something—as he wanted to marry Helen Watson—his tenacity and personal force were

irresistible. He pursued with the sweetness of a kitten and the
ferocity of a lion. He didn't give up until you gave in. Watson
swallowed his doubts and tried to listen to his wife, who told
him to be happy because Helen was happy. When Helen graduated from medical school and married Winter, her father
treated them to an old-fashioned grand tour of Europe and
Asia for their honeymoon.

As Winter got older and more successful, the stories he told
about his childhood made it out to be increasingly sordid and
difficult. He used to say he was a guttersnipe. In fact, his father
was a doctor in a lower-middle-class community in Baltimore.
Although the Winternitz family didn't go to synagogue, they
were part of the Jewish immigrant community, and the family
was run with the strictness of a middle European home. Children were treated like servants, and their father was waited on
and obeyed. His starched collars were sent to Paris to be prop-
erly laundered.

By the time he married in 1913 Winter was already famous at
Hopkins for brilliant research and unorthodox teaching
methods. His challenging questions—so different from the
droning lectures featured by most professors—kept classes on
edge. "Winternitz always seemed like an animal about to
spring," wrote one student. "Alertness in his class was essential
for survival." In 1917, Winter was appointed professor of pathology and bacteriology at the Yale University School of Medicine.

Yale was an ailing school with a bleak prognosis, housed in
one laboratory building and a few shacks. Two professors had

resigned and another had been transferred out. There were fewer than fifty students, culled from sixty-eight applicants. Winter's prodigious energy—Yale president Angell called him a "steam-engine in pants"—was immediately apparent. In 1920 he was appointed dean of the medical school. Within a few years he quadrupled the school's endowment, began an ambitious building program of laboratories and classrooms centered around an Institute of Human Relations where medicine was studied in conjunction with other disciplines, and completely revamped the curriculum. The widely copied "Yale plan" allowed students to cut almost one thousand hours of required classes if they could pass a rigorous biannual examination. Winter taught that each patient must be studied and treated as a whole human being—not just a conglomeration of symptoms.

Yale's aging pundits sat up and took notice; many were outraged. Almost everyone who taught at Yale in those days had gone to Yale as an undergraduate. Reactions to this outspoken outsider were extreme and divided, but in 1925, at the end of his first five-year term as dean, the Yale medical school faculty overwhelmingly recommended his reappointment. Winter was an intruder in the stately Yale administration, and he used this. He seemed fearless about doing things efficiently and quickly—rather than by Yale standards or according to Yale traditions. At the same time he hired the Protestant establishment's best and brightest, enlisting men who had the credentials he lacked in his crusade to build the best medical school in the world.

More than five hundred applications a year poured in, and

Winter interviewed each applicant in person. The interviews were as volatile as the dean. One applicant had a heavy book thrown at him as he approached Winter's desk. He caught the book, and won admission. As the medical school took shape on a hill near the undergraduate campus, Winter began a hectic schedule of speaking all over the country, both on his academic miracle-in-progress and on his research. He had done definitive work on war gases as a captain in World War I, and he had written *The Pathology of Influenza*, a book that helped change the study of pathology from an examination and description of dead tissue to a study of tissue which encompasses experiments on the nature of disease. Winter's classes at Yale were legendary, and his weekly department meeting, when he applied his irreverent technique to other professors as well as students, was a standing room only event.

In the eye of the hurricane he had created, Winter put in a five-hour-a-day teaching load and did two to three hours of research in the Brady laboratory. During the summer he took his research up to Treetops, where he set up a laboratory in the garage and wrote his annual reports. A group of his students built a white frame building at the edge of the orchard for his experiments, with a plaque inscribed *Hic Est Locus Ubi Hiems In Aestas Reperit* (This is where Winter comes in the Summer). The building with its high lab bench and working stools is still there. My father used to write in it sometimes, typing in the midst of old petri dishes and lab tools and unused canisters of chemicals. Now dead leaves and years of dust cover the bench. The stools are rusted into position, and Winter's old sofa is a home for field mice.

I never saw Winter teach, although his terrifying didactic

method was not restricted to the classroom. Even in conversation with his grandchildren he would let loose a stream of rapid-fire questions which left some of my cousins baffled or in tears. There were never right answers. When we produced wrong answers, he would stamp his stick on the ground and demand more. Winter was never interested in answers—he was interested in further questions.

As Winter became famous for his research, his teaching, and his administrative genius, he became even more famous for his abrasive manner and his public temper tantrums. His sharp tongue wasn't left behind at the Brady labs when he went home at night; his children often felt it. On meeting one of his son's girlfriends he remarked, "Any lab assistant of mine could have put together a better looking woman than *that* with two old crows and a lathe."

As he got older, he tried harder to control the inner pressures that drove his talents but that also triggered his impatience—with imperfect success. When my father met him in 1938, Winter was an imposing figure who wore a proper felt hat and a bow tie with his custom-made suits. His face was dominated by prominent dark eyes. "The success he has made of his work made him seem over-confident, even ferocious," my father wrote. "The insecurity of his personal life made him seem youthful and lost."

This is one story told about Winter: A student had married a girl below his social station—a girl from the wrong side of the New Haven tracks. His mother, a queen of New Haven society, succeeded in getting him to leave his new wife and then brought him to the great Dean Winternitz for chastisement. "Madam," Winter told her. "There *isn't anyone* below your son's social station in life. They don't come any lower than a skunk who will marry a girl and then desert her because Mama is annoyed." Both mother and son left in a hurry.

During their first New Hampshire summers, in 1922 and 1923, Winter and Helen rented a cottage in Bristol, a small mill town near Newfound Lake. When their young children trooped down the hill for a swim, a dog named Bruce from a neighboring farm barked at them. Winter bought them a sad-eyed collie cross, with shaggy brown and white fur, which they named Mutsy. Mutsy was later joined by a pit bull named Ace.

When a fifty-acre tract of land on the southern slope of Peaked Hill next to Bridgewater Mountain came up for sale, Winter and Helen hiked up the dirt road and bushwhacked in through the underbrush to an abandoned foundation at the bottom of a broad pasture. My grandmother climbed a tree and looked down from her branch toward the lake and the mountains beyond it and toward the hills to the south where the distant white steeple of the church in Alexandria lies in a fold of wooded land; she fell in love with the view.

Treetops was carved out of the woods on that steep hillside. Grandpa Watson paid for it, and Winter and Helen populated it with their five children—my mother and her sisters and brothers. It was to be a family place with organized activities and the discipline of manual chores—the children even wore informal uniforms, middy blouses for the girls and sailor shirts for the boys. Gardens were laid out. An oval lawn was built of boulders and earth, and a driveway was graded around its perimeter.

The cottages were constructed with open stud walls and no insulation, each with one or two bedrooms and a small bathroom, and a porch for looking down at the view. Above the oval lawn they put up a main house, with a central kitchen, an indoor dining room for cold days, and a dining porch. Each cottage was named after the trees that grew around it—apple, balsam, pine, hemlock, birch, spruce, and bushes.

Treetops was a pastoral paradise, but it was run more like a work camp than a resort. Vegetables had to be picked, cleaned, and washed before children went to the lake. The chickens and turkeys had to be fed, their houses cleaned and eggs gathered. Sunny afternoons were spent in the gloom of the cement-floored laundry and canning shed, brushing and scraping the corn, sterilizing bottles, and stirring huge vats of cooked fruit for jam—with jobs assigned to each child according to age. Work Is Pleasure was Grandma Watson's favorite motto.

At the end of each day the children were herded down to Pine, where Grandpa and Grandma Watson always stayed. Seated in a circle on the hard floor as the girls sewed and the boys tied up bundles of kindling, they were treated to long readings from improving texts selected by Grandma Watson from the *Reader's Digest* and the *National Geographic*, or to Grandpa Watson reading from his favorites: Dickens and Shakespeare.

Above the property where Treetops was taking shape, a farmer named Pete Charron had a red farmhouse on the hill. Charron was a sage, a tall man with a Yankee face, who was a good builder and an inspired mason. He had a naturally elegant country taciturnity which used to thrill and amuse my mother's family. When someone asked him how many trees he had lost in the storm of '38, for instance, he paused and answered, "Well, I know where they all are." When my Aunt Janie backed the family Studebaker into her brother Stevie's brand-new roadster and dented the door, Pete Charron straightened it out and interrupted Stevie's screaming tirade about his sister's lack of brains to show him that the door still worked. "But, but . . ." Stevie sputtered. "Look at that dent!" "Oh that," replied Pete, "well, it won't bother you much once you forget about it." It was Pete Charron who took the Winternitz brothers, Tom and Bill, as his charges and filled their summer days with building projects and incidental lessons in botany and woodsmanship.

Below the property, a Latvian immigrant named Peter Weesul tilled the pastures around the farm where he lived with his wife and daughter. Peter Weesul was an inspired gardener. He seemed to be able to talk to the soil more easily than he could talk to people. His silences sometimes suggested that he cared more about the land and the plantings than he cared about its owners.

Watson and his son-in-law Winter, both with their substantial egos, were out to create a dynastic compound in the wilds of Grafton County. Together they planned and built a place that would be the seat of family mythology for generations—and the proving ground for their separate philosophies of child rearing and their beliefs about human nature.

Otherwise, they pretty much hated each other. Although they were each self-created, they had created very different selves. Winter was a short, angry man, who worshipped science and adored power and wealth in all its manifestations. Watson was tall and effortlessly handsome with a mane of white hair, and *his* childhood experience with poverty had left him uncomfortable with money and power. Although he had money, more than Winter would ever have, he didn't care about it. His basic philosophy was also in direct conflict with Winter's. Winter was an atheist who believed that the proper study of mankind was biological and medical phenomena. Watson was intensely spiritual with a lot of vague ideas about reincarnation and the harmony of the Universe. He saw nature as God. Winter saw nature as a thoroughly explicable series of chemical changes.

Their differences in temperament and beliefs led to radical differences in style, which influenced the creation of Treetops. The simple frame cottages at the top of the hill were Watson's domain. He disliked anything fancy. In fact, at the end of his life, he got in trouble with the IRS, whose agents refused to believe that a man of his standing would have a modest cottage as his primary residence. He did. Down the hill, below the orchard, Winter planned his sort of house for Helen—the Stone House. Watson had designed the cottages himself. Winter hired a fashionable New York architect, Henry Pelton, to design the Stone House, an elegant modified saltbox with a double-story living room, tiled terraces, and a lily pond. At the top of the hill, the work was done by amateurs. Looking up at the ceilings of the cottages, you can still see the small footprints and paw prints of the naughty children and dogs who ran across the pine tongue-and-groove boards as they lay on the grass waiting to be mounted on the roof beams. In the Stone House, an ironsmith was hired to create wrought iron sconces, railings, and lamps. There were real ceilings and insulation and a wood-burning furnace in the cellar for cold days.

But in spite of their differences and the friction between them, the two men were bound together by their love for Helen, by their ambitions for Treetops, and by Grandma Watson, who acted as a go-between.

🦋

It is 1989, and sitting in a darkened room in the Bell Laboratory Archives in Warren, New Jersey, I watch as my mother and her sisters and brothers sit in a restless circle around my great-grandfather on the 16-millimeter screen. The film was made in 1929 by a friend of Grandpa Watson's, who thought it would be nice to make a movie of the great old man demonstrating the telephone to his adoring grandchildren. The children are antsy and the demonstration heavily choreographed, but everyone is true to character. Buff grabs the receiver to take a closer look. Jane tells everyone what to do. Tom trips over Mutsy, who is lying on the grass. My mother, Mary, rangy and graceful and looking as if she came from another family, stands slightly removed from the scene, scratching a mosquito bite on one long leg with her other bare foot.

My great-grandfather Watson's papers are kept under guard in a single-story, corrugated iron building in the New Jersey woods off Route 78. Bell has grown so large that its archives alone are a full-time business for dozens of workers. There is Grandpa Watson's logbook from March 1876 (no mention of the spilled acid) and dozens of his letters in flowing, old-fashioned script, all carefully filed.

"Wait until you get to the best part," the archivist says as I watch the movie. The Bell archivists and researchers have taken on my search for the past as their own, and a small audience has gathered in the darkened room. With the jerky, comic movements of a silent movie, Grandpa and Grandma Watson two-step out of Pine cottage and then walk with a weird rapidity reminiscent of the Marx Brothers up to Apple, where the children await the great demonstration. Later, Grandpa Watson proudly shows off the chicken houses and the turkeys for the camera. A rooster preens while the five children loll against a fence and make faces at each other.

"The best part" is the footage shot from the rocky shore of Newfound Lake; the five children dive from a board on the raft and swim in toward the camera. Ace, the pit bull, gets left on the raft, but after some whining and coaxing, she dives in, too, and heads for shore, leaving a V-shaped wake in the clear water.

"Hardly anything has changed!" my mother says proudly, when I show her a videotape of the movie. It's true. There are fewer hydrangea bushes around the oval now, the flower beds are overgrown, and many of the lake views have been blocked out by pine trees on the hill, but Pine looks exactly as it did when I swept the floor, loosened the fuses, and closed it for the winter this year—sixty years after the movie was made.

Treetops has always been a place where the past is very much alive. The old ways there are sometimes inadvertently, sometimes desperately, preserved. When my mother and her siblings visit it now, they occasionally revert to what they were as children. They pick and clean vegetables. They take marathon swims and mountain climbs. They tell stories. They sit around and talk nostalgically about their father Winter's human Rototiller—five children crawling through the dirt with their noses to the ground. Their voices change, becoming higher and lighter. Sometimes, as they clean a cottage or mow the lawns or work in the kitchen, you can hear them talking to themselves— they seem to be talking to the dead.

THREE

THE LIVES OF the men in my family seem to be shaped by cause and effect. Their successes and failures are the direct and deserved result of their talents and character. The lives of the women are harder to understand. What happened to them—including early death, incarceration in a mental hospital, and debilitating powerlessness—seems to have less to do with who they were than with the times and their family and the men they happened to end up with.

In Grandpa Watson's autobiography, he mentions his wife only once—to note that he met her at Kimball's Inn. There are pages on the beauties of the Cohasset shoreline and the ecstatic hours he spent daydreaming on the ledges above the beach, but Elizabeth Kimball Watson gets less than a sentence. Yet in most of the photographs of Watson as a Great Man, she stands loyally next to him. In the 1929 movie made at Treetops, Grandpa Watson is always on camera. Grandma is an incidental presence in an old-fashioned long dress, bustling around and getting everyone some lemonade.

In my family, attitudes toward women are complicated and confusing—and the women tend to be complicated and confused. Women are expected to wait on their men. They are also, beginning with my mother's generation, urged to get advanced degrees, have careers that are useful to society, and learn to support themselves. At the same time, they are supposed to bear and raise children. No one seems to notice that there is a conflict.

Thomas Watson, Dean Winternitz, and my father were all natural autocrats—family tyrants. All three came from families where there wasn't enough money. All three had childhoods dominated by deprivation, loneliness, and big, big dreams. I think that each one of them had, at some point, looked around at the ordinary family into which they were born and realized that some terrible mistake had been made—they didn't belong in that dowdy family at all. They were too smart and savvy to imagine themselves the mistakenly adopted, mistakenly abandoned scion of some royal family, but that was how they felt. Instead of waiting for their true, royal parents to show up, however, they each went out into the world and claimed their birthright. Each one wove a story around himself, inventing a character, a career, and a set of interests that were entirely apart from his family's limited expectations. This was their most inspired storytelling. So it happened that my father, born into a family of failed businessmen and golfers, decided to be a writer; that my great-grandfather, born in the Salem livery stable, decided to be a scientist and scholar; and that my grandfather, born into a poor Jewish family in Baltimore, decided to set the genteel Protestant world on its well-shaped ear.

Although these men weren't related to each other by blood, their connection is clear. My grandmother married a man like her father, and my mother, in turn, married a man like *her* father. Their external circumstances were different, but at heart these three men were the same.

❧

Grandpa Watson had hoped that his daughter Helen would marry someone from an established, well-bred background. But of course, like many strong women, she married a man who made her father bristle. When Helen and Winter came back from their honeymoon, Winter returned to Johns Hopkins, where he resumed his privileged teaching position under the protection of his mentor, Professor William Welch. Instead of beginning her own medical career as a practicing doctor, in 1914 Helen gave birth to her first child, named Elizabeth after her mother. By the time Winter decided to go to Yale in 1917, Helen had three children—Elizabeth, Thomas, and Jane—and a household to move to 210 Prospect Street in New Haven. In 1918 she gave birth to her fourth child in four years, my mother, who was named Mary Watson after her paternal grandmother. Winter was immediately taken up with the excitement and challenges of his new job. In 1919 Helen was pregnant again, but she had a miscarriage. Then in 1920 she gave birth to the fifth child in six years, a son, and she named him William Welch Winternitz.

Winter's rapid and astonishing achievements in his first years at Yale absorbed him completely. Back home, on the other side of town, his young wife was struggling to care for five children under six.

Her husband adored her—but he was obsessed with his work. She had no work. Instead, there were colds, colic, chicken pox, as well as infections and scarlet fever—both serious illnesses in the days before antibiotics. There were servants, but the servants didn't bear the children or nurse them. Isolated by her husband's success and her own fertility this fiercely intelligent woman was suddenly catapulted from an independent life into a life of pregnancies, painful deliveries in the days of primitive anesthesia, high risks of infection and postpartum complications, and the squalling chorus of five children's demands on their mother. Biology had become destiny.

Until birth control was widely available, women's lives were absolutely controlled by the necessity of having children. Birth control was used by some women in the 1920s, but it was illegal. As late as 1929 there were police raids and mass arrests at Margaret Sanger's birth control clinic in New York City. Diaphragms still had to be smuggled into this country from Germany, hidden in oil drums. This was not the sort of thing that Dr. Helen Watson Winternitz would get involved in, and certainly not anything her husband would condone.

Ironically, Helen's medical background may have helped keep her from even considering the use of birth control. The American Medical Association was against birth control, citing it as a threat to personal morality. Typically, Dr. George Kosmak, a prominent gynecologist and later the editor of the *American Journal of Obstetrics and Gynecology*, told his colleagues in an address on the subject that birth control advocates were "radical socialists" and "anarchists" out to libel the medical profession. According to the medical establishment, the only proper method of controlling pregnancies was abstinence—or in cases where control was essential to health—sterilization.

Helen weakened with each successive child while her husband grew stronger as he embarked on the new accomplishments that would make him one of the most renowned teachers and administrators of his time. The lab and the medical school took up most of his days in New Haven, and he traveled frequently to lecture or go to conferences.

※

My mother doesn't talk very much about her mother. She has two photographs of her: one, a wedding picture of a handsome woman in a full-bosomed pearl-and-lace white dress, hangs in my mother's dressing room in the house where she lives in Ossining; the other of the same woman in an elegant day dress with pearls, looking stern and slightly amused, hangs above my mother's bed in Hemlock, the cottage where she usually stays when she goes to Treetops.

"Oh," my mother says breezily on the telephone, when I ask her about her mother. "I was the child she didn't want."

"Surely not," I say.

"She told me that," my mother says in a matter-of-fact tone. "She wanted another boy to play with Tommy. She was very disappointed when she had a girl, she wished she hadn't had me."

"Did she just want boys?" I ask.

"Oh no. She loved having Buff and Jane. She loved to dress

them up with a big blue ribbon in Buff's hair and a big pink ribbon in Jane's hair. There wasn't even a color left over for me."

"How could she tell you that?"

"They didn't think children had feelings in those days," my mother says nonchalantly, as if we were talking about the amount of lemon juice to put in a mayonnaise recipe. "They thought children were just like little animals. They thought you could just tell children anything that came into your head. . . . COCO!" She suddenly interrupts herself with an order to her dog. "GET off there this minute!" *Now* she sounds indignant.

"Mother, I fall for you / through a brown slick of photographs," my mother wrote in a 1980 poem titled "Remains,"

> Bride full lavish
> lace sails, fat
> roses drooping
>
> Babies slipping
> her arm like sleepy
> fish
>
> I fall to the hill room where
> bone thin and brown as earth
> you raise again the body of despair
> and pain.

By 1925, Helen's physical condition was much more critical than anyone realized.

"We had a wonderful time," Winter wrote Helen's father, Grandpa Watson, in a chatty letter that gives the first hint of problems, "and the more I see of Treetops the more I am inclined to stay there all the time." It was April, and he and

Helen and two of the children had gone to stay a few days in the rudimentary cottage called Balsam.

When we got to Manchester it began to rain and therefore we had to drive very slowly, but we reached Bristol early enough to get some provisions and then proceed up to the camp. . . . The weather was pretty bad while we were there. It rained and on Sunday night it snowed so Monday morning when we awoke there was four and a half inches of snow over everything. . . . It was a beautiful sight to see this softly clinging snow. We went to bed with the chickens and got up at daybreak, for we had no lights . . . and we had to do the cooking out of doors because we were unable to use the stove as there was no water. But these hardships seemed minor and the real joy of being there in the outdoors was great. Both children seemed to benefit tremendously and both Helen and I felt much better for our outing. Unfortunately Friday morning Helen woke up with a sore throat and by afternoon was very sick indeed with follicular tonsillitis. I was home with her all Saturday and Sunday and am glad to say she is ever so much better. Her temperature at noon was only slightly above normal, and her general condition was very much better. It is only a matter of a day or two before she will be herself again.

But it was more than a matter of a day or two. Helen felt better and then she was sick again. No one really knew what was wrong. She lost weight, had trouble breathing, and spent more and more time in bed. She had the best medical care that could be found, but each recovery was followed by a relapse. By 1928, when the Stone House which Winter had built for her was ready to be roofed, she was too sick to travel to Treetops for the summer and Winter stayed with her in New Haven. The five children spent the summer at Treetops with Grandpa and Grandma Watson.

In 1929, Balsam burned to the ground. Winter decreed that knowing this would be too distressing for the ailing Helen to bear. He had the cottage rebuilt in every respect, even replacing the furnishings with duplicates as best he could and replanting the shrubbery exactly as it was before. She would never know that there had been a fire.

Winter's only confidante, the person to whom he poured out his grief and depression at what was happening to his beautiful wife, was Helen's favorite child—her son Tom, who was away at boarding school.

"Mother has had a pretty bad day today," he wrote Tom in February 1930, along with liberal scoldings about Tom's spelling and his infrequent letters.

"When I reached home in the evening Mother seemed fairly happy," he wrote in March. "I read to her for a while and prepared something for her to eat at about 10:30. . . . Finally I opened her window and fixed her up for the night at about 11 o'clock. She slept about two hours and then woke up in pain. I think that for the first time in my life I could not get myself together. I seemed to hurt all over and it took me half an hour to do what I should have done much more rapidly. Finally Mother got to sleep again. . . . I expect the girls will come home this evening. . . , but I shall not see them tonight for I must go to Bridgeport to speak—another chore."

Winter wrote hundreds of letters to his children. He often wrote each child two or three times a week—and he expected them to reciprocate. Most of his letters are tedious daily logs, telling what he had for dinner, what his travel plans were, and what each of the other children were doing. In the 1930s he started copying each letter he wrote and sending it to all the children, rather than writing separate letters to each child. Finally, he just gave up being personal and produced a weekly Bulletin. But his letters to Tom in 1930 are both personal and written to Tom alone.

"That was a fine trout," he wrote, toward the end of April 1930. "I cannot tell you how glad I am that you sent it to Mother. . . . This evidence of your love for her will remain as a deep, bright spot in your life always. You are the apple of her eye. . . . It is on this account that I am so hesitant to write you today because I am sorry to say that Mother is awfully ill and it is quite possible that I shall have to send for you even before you get this letter, because I want you to see her again."

These frank letters, with their appeal for friendship and their reassurances, are unique in Winter's correspondence. He was not a man to talk about his feelings or to admit that he couldn't get himself together. His idea of an affectionate gesture was a slap on the back, or a challenging question. In the forty years of his correspondence preserved in the Yale archives, there are no other letters like these to his fifteen-year-old son in the days around his wife's death.

Tom says he hardly read the letters. He was preoccupied with schoolwork and worried about his mother. When I tell him now that these letters from his father are personal and moving, he shrugs his shoulders. There was terrible grief in Winter's outpourings, and terrible irony. For all his knowledge, for all his belief in science, and for all his passionate love for Helen, he had to watch helplessly as life ebbed away.

"I'll never forget that day," my mother says, when I ask about her mother's death. Her voice cracks. "I don't think Daddy ever believed she could die." It was April of 1930. My mother and her brother Bill were the only children living at home; the others were away at boarding school. The pain in the house, as their mother had more and more trouble sleeping—more and more trouble breathing—enveloped them all like a cloud.

"When it happened, my father came down the back stairs to tell us. He was holding her black cat, the cat that had slept on her bed the whole time she was sick. The look on his face was awful, it was worse than sadness. . . ." She stops talking.

Even now, in a family of doctors, no one seems quite sure what was wrong with Helen—what sent her to bed in 1925 and finally caused her death in the early spring of 1930. Her son Bill, a doctor, says it was nephritis, or kidney disease. Her daughter Jane tells me it was a blood disease—streptococcus septicemia—and that they found the cure with the discovery of sulfa drugs a year later. My mother still thinks it started with a chill her mother got in the summer of 1924, when she and Winter went into town to help victims of the Great Bristol Fire. What is sure is that Helen's death combined with her long, painful illness left scars on the family and on her children which have never healed.

"Mary's mother was seriously ill prior to her death in 1930," Winter wrote on my mother's application to Sarah Lawrence College. "Mary and her younger brother were at home for a considerable part of these five years as the other children were away at boarding schools. Even in the summer, her contact with her mother was small, and during two summers her mother and I were not able to join the children in the country. It is needless to say that the children's social opportunities were greatly restricted on account of these unavoidable circumstances. I think Mary became somewhat self-contained and perhaps a bit introspective."

Because of Helen's illness, her parents, Grandpa and Grandma Watson, took on a large part of the raising of their grandchildren. It could not have been an easy duty for them, especially during the years when they knew that their child was dying. The photographs of Grandpa Watson after her death show that he suddenly became an old man. His handsome face is drawn with sorrow, and he looks as if he's about to weep. He only outlived her by four years.

Even in the months after Helen died, Winter couldn't quite believe what had happened. He continued the reconstruction of Balsam. "Mother never knew the house burnt down," he wrote his son Tom proudly, although since she had never seen the rebuilt Balsam it's not at all certain that Winter's ruse would have succeeded in fooling her. In fact, when Helen was shown the 1929 film of Treetops, in which the burned-out foundation of Balsam is scrupulously kept off-camera, she asked again and again, "Where is my house? Where is my house?" But at least rebuilding it allowed him to think he was doing something which might have made her happy. "I am very glad," he continued in the letter to Tom, "because I know it would have pained her to think of all the things we gathered from here and there to make the place attractive. Of course . . . I shall keep on gathering them until the house is as complete as possible." The little things he gathered to comfort and deceive a dead woman he loved are still in Balsam. A few rush chairs, an antique sewing box, a print of Windsor Castle, and a studio portrait of the five children. My mother is a little girl with bowl-cropped hair, Elizabeth and Jane wear pinafores and huge Alice-in-Wonderland bows. All of it—the clothes, the posed children, the furniture, and Winter's desperate, romantic gesture of restoration—seem to come from much further away than sixty years.

At Treetops, we're always doing battle with the passage of time. The reconstruction of Balsam after the fire, which in some way did turn back time—a heartless time which could not be turned back enough to keep Helen alive—may have been the first blow in a continuing war between my family and the inexorable march of the months and years.

FOUR

In the months after Helen's death, the widowed dean suffered severe depression and loneliness. He buried himself in his work and tried to forget. But Winter was irrepressible and, rather quickly, he began to bounce back—certainly too quickly for his children's taste. He fell headlong and hopelessly in love with the redoubtable Mrs. Pauline Webster Whitney, a prominent New Haven socialite and the widow of Stephen Whitney. Mrs. Whitney was everything Winter wasn't; she had been born to privilege and married wealth and society. She was a member of the New Haven Lawn Club and every other club that counted. She was a tireless charity organizer, and she dined with and influenced the men who automatically wielded the kind of establishment power that Winter had to scrap and slave to get. She lived in a world where whom you knew, whom you were related to, and whom you went to school with were more important than what you had done. Everything about her, from her prejudices to her elaborate hats, indicated that there was just one way anyone who was anyone behaved—and that she was the epitome of that behavior. Unlike many of her type, however, Polly Whitney also had a sharp wit, and her assessments of people, delivered in her relentlessly upper-class drawl, were often both true and funny. She was restless.

This seemingly immovable object—the fully decked-out society woman—met with its irresistible force one afternoon in New Haven at the junction of Chapel Street and York Street. Winter, whose driving was always very exciting because he never paid attention to trivia like road signs, went through a stop sign and drove his Buick right into Mrs. Whitney's highly polished maroon Packard. Winter got out of his car and watched as Mrs. Whitney, dressed as usual in a designer suit, expensive shoes, and a large hat, slowly, scornfully emerged from hers to see what lower order of human being had caused her this inconvenience. She looked him up and down, and recognized him. "So, you're Dr. Winternitz from the medical school," she said, "who's supposed to be so *smart!*" Winter had met his match.

Within a year of Helen's death, their courtship was going full tilt. Stephen Whitney had died suddenly, also in the spring of 1930, and Polly (as Mrs. Whitney was called) had lost her mother a few months later. Winter mounted one of his all-out campaigns, and Polly couldn't resist.

One summer night at Treetops in 1931, Winter woke the children at 2:30 A.M., loaded them into the open rumble seat of his Buick roadster, and drove five hours over the mountains to Portland, Maine, to breakfast with Mrs. Whitney and her children, who were spending a night there to break their annual pilgrimage from the social life of New Haven to the even more rarefied social life of Northeast Harbor. After breakfast, he herded the children back into the car and drove them the five bumpy, windy hours home. They're still furious.

Later that summer, Mrs. Whitney and *her* children, on their way home from Northeast, were welcomed at Treetops by Winter, playing lord-of-the-manor—a manor that, after all, had been provided by his father-in-law. He showed her where the tennis court was going and took her for a ride on the lake in the canoe. For once, both Whitney and Winternitz children agreed on the effect of the courtship on their parents—it was ridiculous. "It's the only time either of them was ever out in that canoe," Janie Whitney Hotchkiss remembers.

Polly Whitney had four children, Stephen and Freddy, both dapper young Gatsby types, the already beautiful and enchanting Louisa—a year younger than little Jane Winternitz—and Janie, the baby, aged ten. The Whitney children were tall, blue eyed, reeking of social confidence, and convinced that the world was theirs. The Winternitzes were short, dark, insecure, brainy, and had learned their manners from a mother who was dying and a father who never had any. The two groups of children were different in almost every respect—looks, values, inclinations, and experience. My mother remembers visiting the Whitney children and having Louisa offer her a hand-me-down peach-colored silk slip trimmed with lace. My mother, who had been used to wearing cotton jumpers and bloomers she made herself under the direction of Grandma Watson, had never seen anything like it. She took it home and hid it in a drawer.

The Whitney household on Trumbull Street was a cozy, friendly place decorated for comfort and luxury. Mrs. Whitney had an excellent cook, and she entertained often. If the Winternitz children thought their father was moving too fast in his involvement with Mrs. Whitney, the Whitney children were appalled at the prospect of their adored mother linking up with this bizarre dean of medicine and his ragtag bunch of children.

But Winter was in love, and since he routinely moved heaven and earth to get what he wanted, his own children's reservations seemed a minor obstacle. They needed a new mother, and he was attracted by the Whitneys' close family and by their dazzling glamour. His own children were beginning to look abandoned. My mother had learned to braid her own hair, but she never got the braids quite even. Her older sister Buff had taken over some maternal responsibilities, but not with great success. There was no one to buy their clothes or see that their shoes fit. There hadn't been a woman—or anyone—running the household at 210 Prospect Street since Helen had taken to her bed in 1925, six years earlier. Perhaps Winter imagined the merging of the two families as a surgical transplant, a transplant that would bring together the worldliness of the Whitneys with the seriousness and intelligence of his own children. The other thing both sets of children agree about is that what happened next was a mistake.

The April 6, 1932, wedding of Dean Milton Charles Winternitz and Pauline Webster Whitney took everyone by surprise—mostly unpleasant surprise. "MEDICAL HEAD CRASHES SOCIETY BY WEDDING SMART SET LEADER," read the headline in the *Waterbury Herald*. "Announcement of the marriage . . . comes as a surprise to society and Yale circles in New Haven. No previous announcement of the engagement or wed-

42

ding plans had been made known," gasped the staid *New Haven Register.* "They've got the brains. We've got the manners," another newspaper quoted Freddy Whitney as saying.

The surprise ceremony was at the Whitney house, and Polly wore a brown tweed suit and a corsage of gardenias. "Mrs. Whitney has been prominently identified in New Haven society and is a member of the Junior League, the New Haven Lawn Club, the New Haven Country Club and the Colony Club of New York." Of course the biggest surprise was for the children, especially the Winternitz children, whose father never could bring himself to explain things even in the best of times.

"I am not at all certain you should be written to," Winter scoldingly wrote his eleven-year-old son Bill, who was away at boarding school in Switzerland, on April 5—the day before the wedding and not quite two years after his mother's death. "Over there having a fine time . . . and never giving us a thought!"

"Jane and Mary went back to New York Sunday afternoon," the letter continues after a description of a family trip to Treetops. "But Elizabeth decided she would stay over until Wednesday. As a matter of fact Jane and Mary are coming back here today, and it is possible that Tom may come too, because we are going to have a little party tomorrow morning which will be associated with your acquiring two more brothers and two more sisters and their mother as a real friend. You probably don't know what I'm talking about so I shall clarify the situation for you. Mrs. Whitney has decided to marry me, and the ceremony will take place early tomorrow morning. We are going to Treetops to christen the Stone House. I am sorry you can't be there, but we should have a great time with most of us at Treetops this summer. . . .

"Now," the letter concludes, "if you are a real sport you will sit right down and write Mrs. Whitney, who will be Mrs. Winternitz tomorrow, a very nice long letter. You can address it to 87 Trumbull Street because we probably shall live there until next fall or until we go to Treetops. . . ." The Stone House, which had been built for Helen, would be furnished and lived in by Polly.

Winter clearly needed a wife, the kind of partner he had missed during Helen's illness and after her death. He needed someone to create a hearth that would be a refuge from the buffeting and overwork of the dean's office, someone to take care of his children, someone to entertain his colleagues, and someone to run the small corporation that his family had become. Polly was very good at all that.

The irony is that Winter functioned best in the years when he *didn't* have such a wife. Winter's glory years were the 1920s, when, as a young man and an outsider, he bullied and cajoled balky foundations, stick-in-the-mud bureaucrats, and nervous faculty into making his vision of a brilliant medical school a famous reality. It was an unprecedented accomplishment in the annals of academia. Even with his beloved wife dying at home and his five children desperate for guidance, Winter had the energy to build his dream out of the unresponsive, anti-Semitic academic clay of the old Yale. He was only forty-seven when he married again, but instead of sending him blazing to new heights, the solution to his problems seemed to dampen his angry fire. He never recaptured the forward motion of that difficult, youthful decade. Maybe the energy went into parties at the Lawn Club. Or maybe it's that what we think we need the most, is often the very thing that destroys us.

"He had an infatuation with those people," my mother says. I had asked her why she thought Winter fell in love with Polly. "He felt inferior, because he was a Jew and because he hadn't grown up in a big house on Prospect Street. He believed in a whole romance about those families—the Owsleys, the Stoddards, the Butterworths—they weren't all nice people, but they *did* have a sense of right and wrong, of how to behave and not to behave. I guess he fell for that."

But for the moment, Winter was in heaven. "As I sit here at my desk," he wrote Bill in Switzerland at the end of April, when he and Polly returned from their Treetops honeymoon, "it requires profound belief to think that I have not been in a dream during this past month or so rather than up in New Hampshire after having been assimilated by and assimilating another family. But facts are facts. Your new mother is a very charming woman, and your new brothers and sisters are very delightful. . . . For the moment I am living at 87 Trumbull Street, and I like my new boarding house more than I can tell you. It has eating alone at 210 Prospect Street skinned to death. This was my former custom, as you know, except on high days and holidays when I was honored by a visit from one or more of your brothers and sisters. . . .

"It is going to be great, Old Fellow," he concludes after three more pages of high-spirited chat, "and I know you will enjoy the new situation just as the rest of us all are."

Winter's children suffered from no such euphoria. They were

angry and distraught, and they did not think their new mother was one bit charming. They didn't like the way she took over the house that had been built for their own mother. They didn't like her high-society manner. They didn't like the way she patronized them. "She was so condescending!" my mother says. They didn't like anything about it. The assimilation that Winter hoped for didn't happen; instead, the two tribes squared off and reached for their weapons. "I soon learned that what Polly said was often very different than what she was thinking," Tom remembers. "You could tell her something, and within ten minutes, she would have distorted it and be using it against you." Tom is sitting in the big wing chair that used to be Winter's in the Stone House. Night is falling as we talk. "There were pitched battles between us and the Whitneys right here on this hill," he says. "I really don't like to come here, because it reminds me of all that."

My mother and her brothers *still* think the Whitneys look down on them, and they *still* resent it. As for the Whitneys, they thought their mother had made a mistake, although they believed they had less to lose. Even so, my mother and her siblings remember them as angry, devious, and aggressive when it came to dealing with the pack of pissed-off, unattractive children whom they were now being asked to call brother and sister.

Freddy Whitney picked on his stepsisters, making fun of their clothes and everything else about them. They were often in tears. Stephen had a different approach. Louisa, the beautiful Louisa, led Tom and Bill around by the nose and treated them like slaves.

My mother and her brother Bill, two handsome people in

their seventies, still sit around the dining room table at Treetops and tell their stories about the Whitneys' snobbishness and the Whitneys' perfidy, each one taking a part and then chiming in as if they were singing a long, sad duet. They talk about the Whitneys' laziness in the vegetable garden and about the time Freddy Whitney visited Bill at prep school in a roadster, impressed Bill's classmates, and then publicly tipped him a quarter as he left. And as they talk, the past slowly eclipses the present—a present in which they are successful, satisfied people—leaving a faint glow of color like a moon in the shadow of the earth.

In the fall of 1932, after the wedding, my mother joined Bill at the École Internationale de Genève in Switzerland. Except for Janie, the Whitney children were also away at school, so the warfare that developed between the two sets of siblings took place during the months when they were all together, in the summer, at Treetops.

FIVE

WINTER NEVER DENIED that he was Jewish, he never denied anything about himself, but he sometimes tried to forget it. He dealt with most insoluble problems by ignoring them, and being Jewish in an anti-Semitic time, in an anti-Semitic profession, in an anti-Semitic community was just another problem. He used to say the first time he encountered prejudice was when he had trouble buying the house for his family in New Haven at 210 Prospect Street. It was certainly not the last.

After Winter was appointed dean of the medical school, Yale president Hadley had to bully the Graduate Club admissions committee into making what would normally have been an automatic nomination to the club—and Winter was the last Jew elected to the Graduate Club for thirty years.

"Dr. Winternitz is a Jew," wrote Yale's next president, James Rowland Angell, in a 1934 letter of recommendation for Tom, which Winter had asked him to write to the Loomis School. "His wife was not. The boy has in his physique the Jewish traits." Tom remembers a series of teas at the Angells' grand house where, unknowingly, he was being sized up to see if he was a fit candidate for Loomis in spite of the characteristics of his race.

In 1923, Yale had introduced an official "Limitation of Numbers" plan, along with Harvard and other Ivy League colleges. Ostensibly to help "balance" the student body, the plan's actual purpose was to keep down the percentage of Jews and Catholics. This was done, with little subtlety, by discriminating against scholarship applicants, by screening based on the application's request for a student's mother's maiden name and birthplace—"this knowledge will give us a more accurate check as to the race of the applicant," explained the dean of admissions in a memo to the president—and through personal interviews. Yale was a prejudiced and xenophobic community. Most full professors and deans were Yale graduates. President Angell was the first president in 175 years not to have graduated from Yale, and his faculty kept him aware of it.

In the academic world, and at Yale particularly, outsiders were less than welcome, and Jews were not welcome at all. To make life easier, some Jewish academics played down or tried to obscure their race or religion. A lot has been written about anti-Semitic Jews and the cultural Pyrrhic victory that allowed the handful of Jews who were accepted in the academic world to stay there.

Winter's case was more complicated. On the one hand, he was incapable of playing down any aspect of himself. He never converted, or changed his name, or pretended for a moment to be anything but what he was—a poor Jewish kid from a Baltimore family. He was proud of it. As often as he could, he told how he had worn shabby clothes, how he had inked his foot so his sock wouldn't show the holes, and reinforced the soles of his shoes with cardboard to pound the pavements selling insurance. On my mother's application to Sarah Lawrence he listed both his parents as Semitic. He never changed his middle European tastes. He loved schmaltzy music and Polish sausage. He put cheese on sugar cookies and butter on cake, and he would drive for miles to satisfy his craving for the sweet mustard with pickles and salt bread he had eaten as a child. He liked to ask rude questions. He never made an attempt to transform himself into anything as pallid and bloodless as a WASP gentleman.

On the other hand, and at the same time, he craved their power and security. "Winternitz was the man who raised the Yale School of Medicine from a dismal second-class institution to one of the finest schools in the nation," wrote Dan A. Oren in his book *Joining the Club: A History of Jews at Yale.* "He would also become almost a caricature of the American Jew striving to become part of gentile society. . . . He presented the New Haven and Yale Jewish communities with stunning evidence that the key to rising in the Yale establishment lay in becoming the 'ex-Jew.' " He married two Protestant women—one of them a princess in the society that sought to exclude him—and his children were sent by their mother to the Congregational Church Sunday School, a few blocks down from Prospect Street. Every Sunday the brood of five would be publicly marched, like little ducklings in their Sunday best, down the hill to church.

We live in an anti-Semitic country. Jewish people are still systematically excluded from certain clubs and screened by real-estate agents who know where these clients will not be welcome. Even in the age of assimilation, there are rigid, if hidden, rules in many Protestant communities restricting admission from outside. Before World War II, the situation was both worse and more open, especially in the medical community. Universities publicly stated their quotas, and as late as the 1950s many medical schools still had these restrictive rules in force.

As a victim of anti-Semitism himself, Winter tried to avoid practicing it, but Jewish students who looked to him for leadership were disappointed. He refused to make a cause out of his own Jewishness or anyone else's. Everyone expected the run-of-the-mill Yale professor to be anti-Semitic and anti-Catholic. Winter was supposed to be different. The medical school policy before Winter arrived had been much more restrictive—and after he stepped down from the dean's office it became much more so again. But because he was Jewish, Winter was criticized for a situation he helped alleviate, if only temporarily. Winter admitted many Jewish students, and trained them within an inch of their lives. He was responsible for hiring the only other two Jewish full professors at the school of medicine before 1950.

Although he was too optimistic to know it, Winter was caught in an historical trap. He was the first Jewish full-time professor at the Yale Medical School, and one of a few in the university. If he stood up for Jews and his own Jewishness, he would not have survived at Yale. He wouldn't have been able to do the things he did. On the other hand, by ignoring his own Jewishness, he alienated some of New Haven's Jewish community and many Jews within the medical profession.

My grandfather saved everything that came across his desk during the thirty-three years he was at Yale. Tuition bills and primary school report cards, brochures from his honeymoon, and top secret reports for the War Department on the effects of nerve gases were all filed away by his secretary, along with every letter he received and carbon copies of every letter he wrote. Torrents of trivial daily information sped through the mails in five—and after 1932 in nine—directions and torrents returned, and he kept it all. These personal papers are stored in ten big cardboard boxes now in the Yale archives and manuscripts collection at the Sterling Memorial Library.

The archives room is at the back, past the temple of Sterling's front desk and the card catalogs where earnest Yale students in jeans and T-shirts flip through their academic chores. The archives and manuscripts room has tight security, but they know me there by now. There is hardly ever anyone else working at the long tables where I spread out my authorized, lined paper (no notebooks are allowed), the folders I want to read, and the photocopies I've ordered. Each photocopied sheet has a reminder about the fair provisions of the copyright law printed on the back along with the Yale seal. *Lux et Veritas.*

All through the winter, the archives room's heating pipes are broken, and a rhythmic, irritating banging of metal on metal echoes through the room as I read the accounts of my mother's college study of poetry and her enjoyment of the cook's spice cake.

"Thank God they finally got the heating fixed," I say to the guard as I leave one day early in the spring.

"Some people say they miss it," she laughs. "They say it helped keep them awake."

☙

Winter's insistence to his children that the new Winternitz-Whitney family was going to be great made no difference at all. The children didn't even bother to disguise their anger. And his loss of control over his family was soon horribly matched by a loss of control over his professional life.

He had made many enemies. "Some thought that Milton C. Winternitz was an inflammatory agent causing 'rubor, calor, turgor, and dolor,' on contact," wrote one colleague when Winter was safely dead. He was an inspired leader, but he was a bully. Other department chairmen did not like being shown up in front of students by having questions fired at them in Winter's weekly meetings.

When men, women, or children were incompetent, Winter blew up. I saw him take people apart a few times in my life—a cop who responded too slowly to Winter's having the right of way, a shopkeeper who didn't have an order ready as promised. He whacked away at dogs who misbehaved—and sometimes at children. Once, when he mistakenly got on a plane from Boston to Montreal, he was able to "persuade" the pilot to make an unscheduled stop in Manchester—one of the few times an airplane has been hijacked using a temper tantrum as a weapon. He had a violent, destructive streak, and as he got older, and his life veered crazily from the course he had laid out for himself, it seemed to get worse.

Winter had no use for patsies or yes-men. At the medical school he surrounded himself with the sharpest minds and the biggest egos he could recruit. He wanted men who could talk back to him, because he knew that the resulting tension would make a wonderful school. "The Dean likes independence as well as courage," wrote one colleague anonymously in the *Yale Scientific Magazine* in 1932. (Many of the articles written about Winter in the medical and university journals were anonymous.) "There is perhaps no better evidence of his own strength and breadth than that he prefers able men. . . . Able, industrious men on the staff have never had to complain of interference with their work, whether their views happened to coincide with those of the Dean or not. Weaker men usually find their lives made so miserable that they prefer to leave." Winter questioned *all* authority, often including his own. Thus he created a great medical school . . . and a political nightmare.

By 1934, his fourteenth year in the deanship, there was severe disenchantment among the medical school faculty— although most of them had been brought to Yale by him and had been honored to come because of him. There had been trouble before in his years as dean, but this time Winter seems to have been distracted. Some of his fight was gone. By late 1934, a group of professors, led by Yale graduate and Skull and Bones man Stanhope Bayne-Jones, had organized against Winter. Bayne-Jones, who had been a student of Winter's at Hopkins and who had been nurtured and finally recruited by Winter to come back to Yale, bent all his energy to unseating his difficult benefactor. He was Winter's opposite. Called "Pinkie" for his ruddy coloring, he was invariably courteous, a thoroughbred Yalie as well as the scion of an old southern family and master of Trumbull College. He presented himself as the antidote to Winter's brusqueness and lack of manners. Winter was an outsider; Bayne-Jones was the ultimate insider. Bayne-Jones was able to enlist a group of faculty members, men who had been so offended by Winter's bad manners that they forgot all about his accomplishments—or men who didn't care about accomplishment in the first place.

In the fall and winter of 1934, this cabal of faculty members went into action. At Yale, the dean was traditionally chosen by the president on the recommendation of faculty. Bayne-Jones began secretly lobbying individual faculty members to line up a majority against Winter's reappointment. Soon Bayne-Jones had collected a threatening number of promises. Belatedly realizing that he faced a mutiny, Winter went to President Angell for help, but Angell, himself an outsider in Yale terms, was unable to change the situation. In a plea to the Yale Corporation Committee on Educational Policy, Winter tried to get the power of appointing the dean taken away from the faculty. It was too late. His third term as dean would be over in June of 1935, and by December of 1934 Winter was anxiously aware that Bayne-Jones and his insider crew intended that his third term should be his last.

On the morning of December 14, Winter got a telegram from Grandma Watson in Florida, where she and Grandpa Watson had retired to the fisherman's shack in Pass-A-Grille. Grandpa Watson, at eighty a hale, still handsome old man, had died during the night—killed by a heart attack. Winter left that morning for Florida to help Grandma with the burial and funeral arrangements, and to make sure she was all right. The minute he was gone, Bayne-Jones called a faculty meeting. By the time Winter got back from burying his father-in-law, a few days later, the faculty had voted to replace him in June when his third term expired. They voted to replace him with Stanhope Bayne-Jones.

What happened next is difficult to understand. Faced with a coup, Winter decided not to fight. He knew that Bayne-Jones would be bad for the medical school (and he was), but he preferred to maintain a dignified silence. It was probably the first dignified silence of his life. He could have caused a huge controversy about Bayne-Jones' tactics, and about his own ouster from the school he had built, and many would have supported him. Even in the fatal faculty meeting, Bayne-Jones had had some trouble winning the votes for Winter's defeat. He could have refused to go, or he could have left Yale and tried to take the best of his faculty with him.

Instead, when President Angell reluctantly and conditionally asked for his letter of resignation, Winter wrote it. Why?

"Why didn't he just burn the place down?" I ask my Uncle Tom. Tom shrugs.

"I don't know. We weren't aware of everything that was happening, but I knew he was very unhappy."

The resignation of Dean Winternitz from the Medical School was big news. Stories appeared in the *New York Times* and the *Herald Tribune* as well as in the local papers and the newsmagazines. The stories said nothing about the coup—and neither did Winter. Hundreds of letters poured into his office at the Brady Memorial laboratory, many of them accusing him of deserting his own school, a school that needed him badly. Winter responded with noncommittal thank-you notes. A few colleagues who knew what had happened wrote a different kind of letter. "I should like to use all the bad signs on my

typewriter to express my opinion of people and things . . . ,"
wrote another Yale dean, Clarence Mendell. "This is a damn
shame. The only kick that I can see, that anybody can have
against you, is that you are a better man than most of us. . . .
We ought to get up and cheer for you instead of sticking pins in
you." "What a stupid loss," wrote James Angell from Columbia
University, "a victory of the philistines." But most people didn't
know what had happened, and Winter didn't tell them. He put
out the story that the load of administrative work had gotten to
be too much for him—*gotten to be too much for him*!—and that
retirement would be a great relief. Strangest of all, he decided
to stay on at Yale and go back to pathology, a position that gave
him a clear view of the incompetent Bayne-Jones guiding his
trim little ship right onto the rocks.

"Polly told him what to do," my mother explains, when I ask
her why Winter didn't fight, why he didn't raise the roof, why
he didn't even make a fuss. "She told him that the right thing to
do was keep his dignity, that the right sort of people wouldn't
make a row, and he did what she said.

"It was good," my mother says. "It was one of the good
things that Polly did for him."

Was it good for Winter, whose great source of strength was in
refusing to curb his instincts, to try and act like the kind of
person he wasn't? As long as he knew he was an outsider, as
long as he didn't expect to be liked or included, Winter thrived.

"He had tremendous respect for institutions," my Uncle Bill
says. "He was loyal to Yale. Maybe that's what kept him there."

Although his children wrote him letters saying how glad

they were that he was retiring because now he would have more time, they remember the winter of 1934 as a time of crackling tension—and one of the few times Polly and Winter worked faultlessly as a team.

The only angry, characteristically direct gesture Winter allowed himself was pathetically small. It was at a farewell party in the Beaumont room of the Sterling Hall of Medicine, the building that most of all embodied his dreams. At the end, when only his friends were left and they had all had a lot to drink, they hoisted Winter up on their shoulders, and with his pocketknife he carved his initials MCW in the wood paneling above the door. It was a sad and silent few minutes, and when he was finished, everyone left the building quietly. The initials are still there.

"It is said that the leader is always a lonely man," said Winter's Yale colleague C-E A. Winslow in a farewell speech to the Dean before the medical alumni association in June of 1935. "The actual situation, as life unrolls . . . is even worse than this. . . . It is a natural human instinct to oppose what one does not fully understand. The pioneer must face, not only lack of comprehension, but defense reactions which constantly place obstacles in the path of progress. The prophet is always rejected by those whom he comes to save. We, your colleagues, have often been the chief barrier to the advance of your vision. . . . The added burden of disheartenment which we placed upon your shoulders must often have been heavy to bear."

After the summer, Winter went back into the labs on Cedar Street and his office in Brady. A group of faculty still adored him, and in each class there were the bright ones who fought back, who made the class sing, and who went on to distinguished careers in medicine—often remembering Winter's teaching as the most important experience of their education. Winter rolled up his sleeves and went back to work. As Chief of Pathology he began a pioneering series of experiments which led to his definitive work on arteriosclerosis. Then, during World War II, he was one of an elite group formed to advise the government on scientific aspects of war. Continuing the research in chemical warfare which he started in World War I, Winter eventually became head of the U.S. Chemical Warfare Service—one of the few civilians in such a top secret capacity. "He enjoyed bossing the generals around," his son Bill remembers. Winter was also involved in the first chemotherapies which used nitrogen mustard gas to alter the white blood cells in leukemia and lymphoma patients. But, although he made a career of snatching victory from the jaws of defeat, Winter never forgot the defeats.

When Winter finally left Yale in 1950, to take a job as head of the medical division of the National Research Council in Washington, D.C., the university showered him with honors. By then he was a legend. When he was finally given the Yale Medal, in 1952, he and many in the audience were moved to tears. Everyone knew, too late, that his fifteen years as dean were some of Yale's finest. "Oldtimers . . . fifty years after the Winternitz deanship would fondly reminisce about the man whom they considered to be the strongest leader that the medical school had ever had," writes Dan Oren. "Later deans would expand the school . . . , but, said the old men, the later deans were mere caretakers."

It's still hard to understand why Winter didn't fight for what he had built at Yale. He loved a good fight. Perhaps it was Polly's influence, as my mother says, or some dream of acceptance. Perhaps something inside him just broke apart at this evidence of human perfidy—evidence of the pettiness of the average soul. Perhaps, after the death of Helen, and the demise of his dreams for Yale, he was just worn out.

When Winter died in 1959 at the age of seventy-four, the autopsy found that his body was riddled with ulcers. There were ulcers on his upper intestine, more on his esophagus, and a series of larger ulcers on his lower intestine. They had been developing for a while; in the end, they perforated his stomach lining and killed him.

❧

When she was a student at Sarah Lawrence, my mother took a summer off from Treetops and went on a bicycle trip through France with a school friend. She loved it. She liked being able to speak the fluent French she had learned in her years at the École Internationale in Geneva, and she embraced French culture, French literature, French food, and the enchanting French landscape. That halcyon summer, before the weight of marriage and children descended on her, but after the helpless, unhappy years of her childhood and adolescence, first with a dying mother and then with a stepmother she hated—remained, for the rest of her life, an island of rich and pleasurable memories.

My mother didn't go back to France for more than forty years. First there was the war, then there was her new family. My father hated France. He said that he hated it because most of his army infantry platoon was slaughtered on the beach at Normandy—by a lucky chance he was transferred out of the platoon and north to a cushy job with the Signal Corps in Astoria, Queens, just before they shipped out—but I think he avoided France because of my mother's infatuation with the country, and because she spoke the language and he didn't.

In 1978, I took a leave of absence from my job at *Newsweek* and went to live with my husband in Fayence, a small town in the Var near Grasse in the foothills above the Riviera. That autumn, my mother finally returned to France to visit us. By accident, her visit coincided with a long-planned visit of my husband's brother and his wife. I had married an older man, and the three visitors were about the same age. Since there wasn't room in the house we were renting, we installed them in a small hotel nearby and hoped for the best.

At first it worked perfectly. My mother and my sister-in-law—both women who had devoted their lives to their house-keeping and child raising, both attractive—immediately found their common ground. Both came from a generation of women who never washed their own hair but had it "done" weekly at a beauty salon, and they went off in search of a hairdresser chatting away about cooking and children and sharing jokes about the difficulties of marriage. My brother-in-law was courtly and protective toward my mother—the woman travel-ing alone—and each day he mapped out journeys for the three of them around the local countryside. They went to Vence and saw the Matisse Chapel. They went to Biot and bought cheese plates and fruit dishes to ship home.

The autumn days—blazing Provençal days, when the air smells of maquis and lavender and the sky is a rosy blue and the wine seems distilled from the warm afternoon air—passed in a pleasant dream of cordiality. I took my mother marketing in the great outdoor bazaar of the Place aux Aires in Grasse, a courtyard surrounded by stone arches where the farmers from all over the Var come to sell their creamy, ripening cheeses and bright, fresh vegetables—shiny purple eggplants and ripe tomatoes that taste like the sun. They sell wine by the jug and jars of black olives and dried herbs and bunches of fresh basil and the powerful marc that they make from the dregs in the wine barrels after the harvest. Afterward, I took her to a tiny restaurant around the corner, where we drank pastis and ate roast chicken with rosemary, and gossiped about my in-laws. There wasn't much to say.

But although my mother and her counterpart *seemed* so much alike on the surface—both had spent most of their lives in affluent suburbs, both had spent most of their lives serving and nurturing men, their husbands and sons—slowly the division between my mother and the rest of her type began to appear like a crack in the ground over an earthquake fault. At first it was almost imperceptible. My sister-in-law had never read many books, and when my mother occasionally started on one of her passionate riffs about French writers or quoted a little poetry with an apologetic giggle, she was met with blankly polite faces. My sister-in-law and her husband didn't speak French, and they were basically wary of the French people, French culture, and especially French food—all things that thrilled my mother.

We began to dread restaurants. My sister-in-law often ordered whatever my mother ordered. She was intimidated by menus she didn't understand, and my mother was her closest link to civilization. But my mother is sophisticated and passionate about food, and my sister-in-law often found it hard to conceal her dismay and disgust when she was served a plate of something that looked or smelled threateningly strange— something that often made my mother exclaim with pleasure— in French. My sister-in-law had heard that the French people eat brains and other unmentionable animal body parts, and she tried to be sure that my mother wasn't ordering anything like *that* before imitating her. My mother, reveling in the eccentric, delicious cuisine of Provence in the autumn, found it hard to resist teasing the other woman about her timorous, fastidious parochialism. A little too hard to resist.

One night, at a restaurant next to the fountain in the flowered central square at Seillans, my mother ordered *ecrevisses*— a plate of tiny sweet crayfish in broth—and my sister-in-law followed suit. As she peered down at the cooked creatures arrayed on her plate, she was clearly horrified. When my mother told the old joke about the Irishman in France who orders *bouillon*, *poireaux*, and finally *ecrevisses à la nage* and when they are served bursts out with, "I drank your dishwater, and I ate your bouquet, but I ain't going to eat your bugs!" none of us laughed.

As my in-laws began to relax in our group conversations, another source of friction quickly surfaced. They started to display a kind of offhand anti-Semitism that was clearly nothing unusual in the neighborhood where they lived. They assumed that they were among friends. In a discussion of real estate, my sister-in-law commented that "the Jews own Miami." When we talked about newspapers, my brother-in-law mentioned, as if it were something we all agreed on, that the *New York Times* was run by "the Jews."

ABOVE: The view from the Stone House at Treetops.

BELOW: Thomas Watson and his wife Elizabeth Kimball Watson.

LEFT: Elizabeth Kimball Watson in 1945 with first telephone from 1876.

BELOW: Helen Watson Winternitz in the 1920's.

Helen Watson Winternitz with two of her children, Elizabeth (Buff) and Thomas (Tom).

ABOVE: Dr. Milton Charles Winternitz (Winter).

BELOW: Winter in his Buick.

ABOVE: The Stone House.

BELOW: Pauline Whitney Winternitz (Polly) in the Stone House.

LEFT: Mary Winternitz in 1925.

BELOW: Mary Winternitz at Sarah Lawrence.

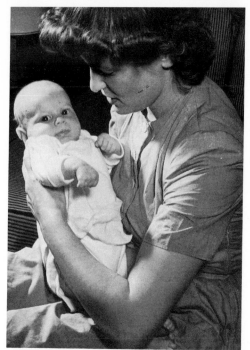

LEFT: Mary Winternitz Cheever and daughter Susan.

BELOW: Mary Winternitz Cheever at Prospect Street with children Benjamin and Susan, and step-mother Polly.

The family at Treetops: (clockwise) Winter, John and Mary Cheever with Ben, Polly, Ethel Whitney, Steven Whitney holding son Dudley, Susan Cheever, and Eugenia Whitney Hotchkiss (Janie).

"Will you tell them that civilized people don't talk that way!" I complained to my husband.

"They're a lot better than they used to be," he said.

"Her father was Jewish, for God's sake," I said.

"Do you think your mother minds?" he asked.

"If she doesn't mind, I mind for her!"

"They don't know any better," my husband said. "I had to tell my parents that they couldn't use the word *kike* anymore."

"There's no such thing as not knowing any better," I said. But for the moment I let the comments pass, and so did my mother.

Late one morning, we all drove to a small town near Draguignon, where one of our French friends had recommended a restaurant. The drive was long and the road sickeningly winding as we swerved over the ridges and through the gorges that criss-cross that part of France. We arrived in the early afternoon. Although it was only about one o'clock, huge sycamores and cedars cast dark shadows over the narrow main street lined with stucco and cinder-block houses.

We sat shivering in the autumn chill at rickety tables on the sidewalk outside the restaurant as we waited to be served. It was a school holiday, and the street had been turned into a drag strip for the local toughs on their fume-belching motorbikes. We had to talk over the din of motors without mufflers and kids shouting at each other. My brother-in-law nervously popped Tic-Tac® candy into his mouth from a plastic box. My mother began to chain-smoke. Motorbikes swerved closer and closer to the curb where we sat in cold discomfort. We seemed to have wandered into some alien and treacherous territory. Suddenly we were American tourists at the edge of the world.

65

Our conversation was barely kept going in spurts and starts by determined effort as we waited what seemed like hours for our lunch. It limped along politely, until my sister-in-law made one of her routine cracks about Jews. This time, in this godforsaken place, with at least another hour of conversation to be got through, my mother decided that things had gone too far. She squared her shoulders and raised her high voice to a strident, accusatory pitch. "I think you should know that *I* am Jewish," she said.

My brother-in-law sputtered an apology, an apology clearly meant for my mother and not for all Jews, and my sister-in-law gasped. After that there was silence. Silence while we waited for our food and silence while we ate it and silence as we drove home, crammed into our little car, through the cold remains of the afternoon to the other side of the Esterel. The jolly clubbiness of the visit had ended. After that there was elaborate, cool politeness. Two days later, my in-laws went home to Connecticut.

SIX

My Aunt Buff—she was called Buff after her own childhood lisping of Elizabeth—was Winter and Helen's oldest child. Blonde and blue eyed, unlike her dark-haired, dark-eyed siblings and parents, she had a short, pointed face and a broad body. In 1931 she entered Vassar College with one of the highest admissions test scores ever recorded. "You know how proud I am of your work," her father wrote her, "and how successful I am expecting you to be—not for my sake, my dear, but for your own."

Four years later Buff was a patient at the Henry Phipps Psychiatric Clinic at Johns Hopkins, weaving baskets and making trays as occupational therapy. "The description of the tray you are making, makes it sound very much better than you may imagine," her father wrote, thanking her for a basket. When she takes her book-binding course, he adds, he will send her a eulogy about him by a Yale colleague to start with.

But Buff may have had mixed feelings about eulogizing him.

Her father had also become her jailer. In the struggle with the doctors for her own independence, Buff must have often felt that her father was on the side of the doctors. "You are pampering yourself," he wrote her after she had been at Phipps five years. Once again she was in trouble for rudeness, for stealing smokes, and for failure to lose weight. "How long do you suppose they will let you stay at Phipps unless you show a greater determination to aid them in your recovery."

The strains put on Buff by her mother's sickness and death and by her father's temperament finally seemed to catch up with her during her first year at Vassar. The summer of 1932, when the Whitney children descended on their new half brothers and sisters at Treetops, destroyed her already precarious balance. Her anticipated success disintegrated into depression alternating with manic periods of drinking, partying, and sexual activity. She began commuting to Silver Hill in New Canaan, Connecticut, for treatment, but during the next summer she was expelled from a Middlebury College program for spending most of the night out with a man.

She dropped out of Vassar in 1934 and went to Silver Hill, but a little more than a year later, Winter decided she should be transferred to Phipps.

Buff's story is not part of our family myth. She is one of the women who sustained extraordinary damage and extraordinary suffering, and no one in the family talks about it. A generation earlier, she might have been tolerated as an "eccentric" aunt or older sister. Her Aunt Esther, Helen's sister, was also extremely unstable. No matter how oddly she behaved, however, she was never incarcerated. The family drew around her, insulating her from society. They set up a trust fund so that her money was safe from her whims. Buff was not so lucky. Being committed to an asylum is itself a heavy blow against stability and self-esteem. If Buff had been born later, her illness might have been diagnosed and treated with drugs. Instead she found herself, in her early twenties, isolated, confined, and shut off from any possible responsibility or social satisfaction.

For a while, her desire to please her father kept their communications friendly. She always adored him. She wrote chatty letters about Baltimore, and he responded with his own boyhood memories and his own Yale gossip. "I had a telephone call from President Hutchins [Winter's friend Robert Hutchins, who was president of the University of Chicago] Monday night. We dropped into Mory's. That was unfortunate because a large group of his classmates were there and before the party was over I was dressed in a fireman's uniform and made an honorary member of the class."

"I suppose you realize that this is the first Commencement Day when I haven't had to march in the procession," wrote the deposed dean to his institutionalized daughter in another friendly letter in 1936. "As I came over here from the dentist I passed the procession at a considerable distance and I was certainly glad I didn't have to participate."

Buff could match her father's insincerity. "Dr. Meyer made rounds and it was very nice to see him," she wrote of the head of Phipps, and one of the more punitive doctors involved in her case. "He asked me how my typewriting was getting along and I replied that it was really getting along quite well."

But Buff hated Phipps. She called it "the hole" and complained of its restrictions and monotony. By 1938, she had begun to feel that the cure selected for her by her doctors and parents—incarceration—was worse than the disease. She precipitated a major crisis by applying to the Katharine Gibbs School in New York on her own initiative. Her typing was good, her Vassar transcripts were acceptable, and she was twenty-three years old.

Her father quickly and vehemently vetoed the plan. During her years at Phipps, his attitude toward her had become increasingly impatient and harsh. The state of medical knowledge concerning mental illness in the 1930s was primitive. Many young women whose problems could not be resolved within the family—and they were often sexual problems— were dispatched to rudimentary "hospitals," "clinics," and "asylums," where treatment usually involved limiting their activity, monitoring their moods, and prescribing sleeping pills. As time passed and Buff didn't seem to get better, her father's letters began to bristle with complaints. She had not lost weight, she had not written him on schedule, she had not taken his advice.

Soon after Winter's marriage to Polly, during one of the summers the whole family was together at Treetops, Polly had come up with her own solution to Buff's problems of instability, sexual activity, and unattractiveness. Buff should be sterilized, Polly said.

Even within the family, no one likes to remember this. "Polly would say terrible things about Buff," Bill told me, grimacing.

"Like what?"

"Just terrible things."

"Did the Whitneys talk about you being Jewish?" I asked.

"Nothing that obvious," Bill said. "Polly went around saying, in that emphatic voice of hers, that Buff should be sterilized. That's what she kept saying after that first summer."

Now, six years later, in the wake of Buff's application to Katharine Gibbs, her father joined Polly in supporting this insupportable suggestion. "The hazard for Elizabeth and everyone else concerned is . . . entirely too great," he wrote Dr. Booth at Phipps. "The problem of sterilization must be considered again, and this time very seriously. Her background is such that any unprejudiced and informed person would feel that sterilization was desirable."

But Buff was as stubborn and strong willed as her father. "I brought up the problem of sterilization," Dr. Booth wrote back. "Elizabeth immediately flew into a rage against you and against us."

Through the spring and summer of 1938, these letters, alternately threatening and cajoling, went back and forth between Winter and his daughter and Winter and his daughter's doctors. "I wonder if Elizabeth has any idea what is meant by sterilization," Winter wrote Dr. Booth. "Perhaps she has an exaggerated idea of the effect it might have on her. As far as I am concerned, I am entirely convinced that in the present state of knowledge concerning the mind, it would be a mistake for Elizabeth to have progeny. . . . Here's hoping she will get to work on the weight problem." And to Elizabeth he wrote, "I have felt for a long time that you would be much safer if you would willingly and intelligently submit to sterilization. This sounds much worse than it really is . . . and I am still hopeful that your intelligence will rise to the occasion."

It was both courage and stubbornness that enabled Buff to salvage some vestiges of dignity and autonomy from the heart-breaking grind of her early years. Finally, her refusal to be sterilized and her general rebellious behavior wore out her jailers at Phipps. Dr. Booth wrote Winter suggesting that the doctors at Phipps had been too patient with Elizabeth. Perhaps she should be transferred to an institution where things were not so easy for her. "In general I do not favor the punitive type of therapy," Booth wrote Winter, "but. . . ."

Then Buff got a break. Winter arranged for her to be transferred out of Phipps to the Butler Psychiatric Hospital in Providence, Rhode Island, where Dr. Arthur Ruggles, an old friend of his who had treated Buff at Silver Hill, had set up a clinic.

"At least Ruggles was a human being," my mother says, her voice rising in defense of her dead sister. "The rest of those men were monsters."

Ruggles' treatment was radically different from the oppressive control exerted at Phipps. Not much was known about manic-depression, but Ruggles made some shrewd guesses about Buff. He allowed her to commute to downtown Providence to hold a job, and she responded right away to this increased independence and trust. There are no miracles, but within three years Buff was successfully holding a job and preparing to marry Walter Thompson, a young chemist she had met in Providence. Within five years she would have her first child—a daughter named Helen.

"As a matter of fact, I think you're the only member of the family I haven't seen recently," her father wrote in a chatty letter in 1942, as if the misery and conflict of the past decade had vanished into thin air. "Mary tells me your apartment is splendid and that . . . you're in very good form."

Buff led a useful and satisfying life. She raised two children, who are both doctors. Her accidental death in 1972, when she was hit by a train roaring through the suburban station at St. Davids, Pennsylvania, where she lived, was a tragedy not a relief. After she left Butler she continued to have unstable times, particularly at Treetops. She threatened to kill the cook one night, and when Winter said she couldn't go on a picnic with the servants, she built a bonfire at the end of the driveway and roasted hot dogs for herself. There were occasional hospitalizations, but her family drew around her, helping with her children and welcoming her back when she was released. In a way, Buff triumphed. She fought for her right to decide her own fate, she fought for her right to have children, and she won.

SEVEN

ONE AUTUMN DAY during World War II, Polly drove my mother and me, age one, up to Treetops. It was evening when we arrived in Franklin—a town twelve miles south of Treetops—and the liquor store was shut. Using her best grande dame manner, Polly inquired at the local grocery store, found out where the liquor dealer lived, and drew her Studebaker up outside his house.

"Give me that infant!" she demanded. My mother handed me over, and Polly, dressed as always in an expensive suit and elaborate hat, pounded on the door until it was opened.

"I have a small infant with me," Polly commanded in her dramatic accent. Night was falling. "I must have a bottle of gin!" Whether it was my infant presence or her tone—the tone of a woman not accustomed to arguments from tradesmen—the man drove us to the liquor store, opened it, and sold Polly her bottle.

If families had flagships, Polly in full regalia—in equal parts

75

majestic and irrational—could have served as the Whitneys'. Descended from an English schoolteacher who emigrated in the 1600s, the numerous and scattered American Whitney clan has become one of the great New World dynasties. There are other famous American names, but Whitney has become synonymous with an aristocratic elegance and a graceful facade that combines the brainless codes of the British upper classes with the urgency and brashness of the colonies.

For the Whitneys, the pattern of life was set at birth by bloodlines and continued by attending the right schools, summering at the right places, knowing the right people, and for the girls especially, marrying into the right kind of family. Polly combined their family chauvinism with their flair. The Whitneys didn't have to feel superior or act superior, they believed. They simply *were* superior.

Good looks, personal style, and conversational wit were the basis of the Whitney code of ethics. Money helped. Life was for amusement, not just accomplishment. Great-Uncle Harry Whitney, who traveled to the Arctic with Admiral Peary, didn't bother to go with the admiral to the Pole. Instead, Uncle Harry stayed behind on the ice cap and spent the year hunting polar bear and musk-ox, hiring a special ship to come for his trophies.

The Whitney manner is unmistakable. My Whitney aunts and uncles and most of my Whitney cousins are tall, small boned, fair, and very good looking. They speak, even in my generation, in an upper-class drawl using an old-fashioned kind of English slang.

"Don't let it rain on your worldlies," my cousin Stephen will say, laughing, as he shuts the doors of my car. They tend to describe people as amusing, or divine, or ghastly, or (worst of all) unattractive. Stephen sells expensive, customized cars to the rich. His brother Frank is the bishop of Chicago. There is a literary agent and a few teachers. All my mother's Whitney stepbrothers and sisters are in The Social Register. Of my Winternitz cousins, eight out of fourteen are doctors and the rest are scientists, lawyers, and journalists.

In my mother's generation, these differences were even more exaggerated. Freddy Whitney became an antique dealer. Stephen taught French at Andover for more than forty years. He is still a stylish man, who wears a broad-brimmed hat and carries a stick and loves to gossip. Janie married Joe Hotchkiss, another New Haven boy. Louisa married the dashing, wealthy Frank Griswold, whose main interests were beautiful women, race cars, and drinking. After he died, she married a Philadelphia businessman who breeds hunting dogs and follows the game, going to Scotland in August for the grouse and the lake country in October for the pheasant.

It would have been hard to find two more different families than the four Whitneys and the five Winternitz children who were thrown together at Treetops in the summer of 1932. My mother and her brothers and sisters had been brought up in a household where science and medicine were twin gods. They were introduced early to the work ethic. Tom and Bill spent hours at Treetops hauling rocks and building walls with Pete Charron; my mother and her sisters heard it preached by Grandma Watson.

The Whitneys, who had been used to glamourous summers with other privileged children, were not pleased to find themselves picking vegetables in the middle of New Hampshire. "I longed for the fleshpots of Watch Hill or Northeast Harbor," my Aunt Janie Hotchkiss remembers. "I thought Treetops was Outer Siberia!" Instead of swimming, sailing, and partying, there was the brambly raspberry patch, where each child was expected to pick a quota of baskets, and the dank canning shed. Polly seemed to take their side. When Winter's cousin Felix Winternitz, a great musician, visited Treetops to play, Polly would, unconsciously, hum a different tune just below the level of the music. The Winternitz children's dog Mutsy would also whine softly. When Felix would stop and ask who was humming, both Polly and Mutsy would also stop and would look around innocently. No one would say anything and the farce continued. Polly also made it clear that, in spite of her love for Winter, she agreed with her children's criticisms of their new siblings.

The result was a children's war. Freddy and Stephen, older and much more sophisticated than the Winternitz children, led the offensive. Beginning in their first summer, Freddy began bitchily picking on his new sisters. Their clothes were ghastly, their manners were abysmal, their bodies were absurd. Most of the time Freddy could quickly reduce my mother and her sisters to tears.

Stephen took a different tack. Buff fell for him and he contemptuously dumped her. She was heartbroken, and the Whitneys made fun of her feelings. With their charm and wit, they enlisted her own siblings against her; by the end of the summer Buff had become a family pariah.

"*They* didn't really like *each other*," my Aunt Janie Whitney remembers about the Winternitz brothers and sisters. What Bill recalls is that that summer pushed his sister Buff over the edge.

If Buff was the worst casualty of the war between the two groups of children, she was not the last.

After dispatching Buff, Stephen went after her two sisters.

"He did the same thing with all of us," my mother says.

"You didn't sleep with him, did you?" I ask, hoping she'll tell me that no, of course she didn't, she told him to go to hell.

"He got me into bed and then felt me all over," my mother says. "Then he came in his monogrammed pocket hand-kerchief. He did the same with Jane."

"Why did you let him?" I ask.

"He was just the most wonderful storyteller," my mother says, as if he had seduced the three sisters with his tall tales. "I remember once a boyfriend of mine came to Treetops to see me, and all he wanted to do was sit up in the kitchen and listen to Stevie tell his stories."

Tom remembers his sisters in tears, and the way the Whitneys made fun of his clumsiness. "I was the stupid one," he says, making a joke of it now, fifty years later. "I couldn't even wave bye-bye until I was seventeen."

Both Bill and Tom were also enthralled by Louisa's beauty. The ugly result of all this sexual power was Buff's collapse, brought on by the brothers and sisters who should have been supporting her, and a coincidental collapse of an entire family's sense of its own worth. My mother never quite recovered. The wounds she sustained from the clash between the two sets of siblings are the ones I know best. She is confused about the role of class and wealth in her life. She has picked up some of the Whitneys' habits—she will ask where someone went to school, or if he or she is related to someone with the same name that she grew up with. On the other hand, she is still contemptuous of their way of life. When she talks about Polly, there's anger in her voice.

As the wife of a celebrated man, my mother has led as glamourous a life as any of the Whitneys. She has traveled like a princess, and become friends with the famous and talented. But her enjoyment of these things has always been tainted by the feeling that somehow they put her on the wrong side of the family. She will buy a lacy, peach silk slip like the one Louisa gave her so many years ago—but she'll have trouble wearing it. She lives in a beautiful, stone-ended eighteenth-century farm-house surrounded by gardens, but she says that what she really wanted was an ordinary house with a backyard and a garage. As she's grown older, her original loyalties, to Bill and Jane and Tom and Buff, have grown stronger. In their old age the four remaining siblings seem to have thrown off, at last, the yoke of doubt and confusion imposed on them by their exposure to their stepbrothers and sisters and the disruptions of their child-hood. Of course, in the meantime, the confusions have been passed on to the next generation.

PART TWO

EIGHT

MY MOTHER MARRIED my father, she says, because everyone told her she should. In her 1941 wedding pictures, she is a beautiful girl in a pale gray silk suit, looking like an animal caught in the headlights of an oncoming car. The thirties, when the grinding poverty of the Depression and the buildup toward the war in Europe made it seem likely that their world was coming to an end, had left my parents' generation intensely insecure. "We just decided not to wait much longer with everything so uncertain," my mother wrote to Winter in explaining her decision to have a small, informal wedding as soon as possible. "Why not take what you can get when you can get it?"

My mother's childhood, a Victorian saga of eccentricity, obsessive genius, madness, and early death, had left her unprepared for life in the twentieth century. When I was born, the strains of caring for a new baby overwhelmed her. The baby nurse, Miss Milkie, was mean and dictatorial, and my mother had no mother to help. My father was away all day. When my mother's older sister Jane arrived, she took Miss Milkie's side and made things worse. Two weeks after we were sent home in triumph from Columbia-Presbyterian, my mother could no longer cope. She and I were both sent back to the hospital. "Poor little Mary," Winter wrote in a letter to a friend. "I'm afraid her life has changed a great deal."

&

My parents met in an elevator in a building on Fifth Avenue. He had been in New York for almost eight years by 1939, and had a small reputation as a promising young writer whose stories often appeared in *The New Yorker*. My mother was a beautiful girl just out of Sarah Lawrence, her brown hair streaked blond by the sun during the summer she had spent at Treetops. She came from a family of doctors and scientists, but poetry and books were what she cared about. She was used to fending for herself in a difficult world, and often for someone else as well. When my father had to borrow money for their first dinner date, it didn't bother her. "I could see he needed taking care of," she said.

My father says that when he saw my mother in the elevator, he knew that she was the woman he wanted to marry. She was working in his agent Max Lieber's office, and he followed her to her desk. They didn't know it then, but both my parents had roots in the sandy soil of Boston's South Shore. My father grew up in a ruined family in Wollaston, Braintree, and Quincy. My mother's grandfather Thomas Watson had lived in East Braintree and later built his Fore River shipyard in Quincy. After my father's father died, his mother moved to a small house on Spear Street in Quincy, just up the street from the Fore River shipyard.

My father fled the South Shore as a young man. It was very beautiful; he was very unhappy there. His flight from home, his wrenching departure from his disintegrating family, appears in many of his stories, letters, and journals. My mother rarely talks about her family history—except when she's at Treetops. In all the times we visited my father's mother in the little house on Spear Street, no one ever told me that my great-grandfather on my mother's side had built the big shipyard at the bottom of the hill, or that my great-grandmother had grown up as the innkeeper's daughter in Cohassett, the next town over. In Boston I was taken to see Paul Revere's house and Old Ironsides and the Old Granary Burying Ground where my distinguished ancestor Ezekiel Cheever is buried, but no one took me to see the recreation of the attic on Court Street where Grandpa Watson and Graham Bell did their early experiments. A faded photograph of my mother's mother was almost all I knew of her before I started writing this book, and my brother Fred wasn't sure what her first name was until a few years ago.

Both of my parents had brutally unhappy childhoods. My father was raised by an old man who never got over the bitterness of losing both his job and his fortune in middle age and an energetic woman who treated her husband with casual disdain as she shouldered the responsibilities he drank to avoid. Neither of his parents had wanted my father—their second son—he was the result of a drunken accident after a salesmen's convention, they told him.

Both my parents moved to New York, embarked on careers that had nothing to do with their families, and married each other hoping to leave behind their memories and start a new life. But the past doesn't get left behind. Both my parents suffered from depressions, ugly memories, and emotional habits left over from the years they wanted to forget.

My father, in his stories and journals and novels, wrote out the past again and again and again. In writing he could allow himself to recollect his pain, his unbearable loneliness, his sense of loss. Even when he was reluctant to write, he often had to anyway. There were children to support, the rent to pay, and food and school bills. By the end of my father's life there was little in his psyche that hadn't been smelted by his enormous talent into fictional form. Like other men in my family, he was able to find salvation in work. My mother didn't have this ability, or this necessity. And so she kept quiet.

When my father began seriously courting my mother, she took him to Treetops. He was fascinated by the beautiful, remote New Hampshire hillside where Dean Winternitz and the former Mrs. Whitney held court. Treetops as it was run by Polly and Winter in the thirties and forties had the kind of throwaway elegance that my father craved—it was also elegance without responsibility. There was a lot of upper-class fuss over flower arrangements and backgammon scores, and a lot of heavy drinking. In the forties, my father grew to love Treetops, and to love the two eccentric, egocentric people who ran it. But at first he was wary.

My mother told him stories. The story about how Winter had taught them each to swim by throwing them off the raft on their fourth birthday. The story about Winter beating Mutsy over the head with a tennis racket until the gut strings of the racket broke, while the children looked on in silent fear.

"As he would put it himself, he was an uncontrolled experi-ment," my father wrote of Winter. "He had no control over his own desires, his own tempers. He could be vulgar, profane, if he was drunk he would tell a pointless obscene story in mixed company, spit into the fire, belch. . . . He loved and he hated. Sometimes they all wished him dead."

My father thought Polly was an arrogant snob whose chil-dren talked like the guest list out of Gatsby. Her mind was filled with trivial memories, he wrote—the face of a chauffeur, the pattern on the Howland's service plates—and her idea of a rustic picnic was a hamper packed by the servants with salmon, fresh asparagus, macaroons, strawberries, and a ther-mos jug of dry martinis. My father saw her as a woman who had never been uncomfortable but whose world was slowly collapsing around her. People didn't live that way anymore. She had never worked for money. "She had been set adrift among her memories like a derelict," he wrote.

For a long time, my father saw his new family from the outside. He was poor (he thought), and they were rich (he thought). Slowly, their charm and generosity wore him down. When I was born, Winter, with a telephone call, had my mother transferred from a crowded ward at Columbia-Presbyterian to a posh private room in Harkness Pavillion. He was unstintingly generous with money, medical advice, and emotional support when my mother had to go back to the hospital.

"I work from nine to one," my father wrote his old friend Josephine Herbst during his fifth summer at Treetops. "I dis-patch a big lunch and then I cut and cart wood, rake hay, make ice-cream and in the late afternoon I go swimming, which I love. Then we go down to Polly's house and drink martinis and admire the view and after dinner we return there and drink coffee and admire the sunset. . . .

"The cast of characters is varied and colorful. The farmer is a communist and loans me copies of a paper called Action. . . . The cook's little girl is sickly and thin-lipped and passes out religious tracts. Mary's sister is as crazy as a bed-bug. Mary's father lectures us on the chemistry of temperament, and Mary's stepmother recalls the evening she was dancing the Castle Walk with Hamilton Fish and tripped on a panier and cracked her skull open."

The sheer beauty of Treetops, the pale crystalline lake, the light so clear it was like a bell chiming in the distance, the limitless view of the mountains, grew on him. He loved the mountain climate where it's cold enough to wear a sweater at night and hot enough to swim in the afternoon. Winter and Polly were always helpful, with presents of Treetops' chickens and ducks during the winter and flowers and vegetables in the summer, with offers to take me in New Haven for a week so that my parents could be alone together, with convenient little checks. When my brother Ben was born, they helped acquire and pay for the nurse, who seemed inexpensive in spite of her high salary, "considering what happened last time," my father wrote them. I went happily off to New Haven while my mother was in the hospital and stayed until she felt strong enough to handle two children. I returned proudly able to recite the Lord's Prayer and "The Jabberwocky." When I turned five, a connection of Polly's materialized to get me into Brearley, the classiest kindergarten in New York.

My father's father was dead, his mother a cranky old woman who ran a gift shop, his older brother a perpetual problem.

Polly and Winter became my official grandparents. They were wonderful to me, and I adored them. Their eccentricities began to seem more interesting to my father, and less threatening. He began writing stories for *The New Yorker* about a place like Treetops and the intricacies of a large family, and the way everyone always sat around telling stories.

"In the summer, when the Nudd family gathered at White-beach Camp, in the Adirondacks," he wrote in 1952, in a story titled "The Day the Pig Fell into the Well," "there was always a night when one of them would ask, 'Remember the day the pig fell into the well?' Then, as if the opening note of a sextet had been sounded, the others would all rush in to take their familiar parts, like those families who sing Gilbert and Sullivan, and the recital would go on for an hour or more."

It was inevitable that my father would be drawn into Winter and Polly's intimate circle, and inevitable that their family dramas would become a resource for his fiction, and inevitable that this should cause trouble, a lot of trouble. My father didn't like to be too close to anyone. He used sarcasm to keep his distance, and courtliness and snobbery. He left home and his beloved brother Fred at the age of sixteen, he told me, because an "ungainly closeness" had developed between them.

The New Hampshire hills against pale blue sky and the dramatic cloud formations reminded my father of Italian painting. At night the sky was alive with stars. Part of New Hampshire's charm is its air of having been abandoned by the farmers who first settled there. Pastures have become forests, and in the meadows there are roses and irises, domestic flowers left behind by the men and women who were driven away by the hardships of growing crops in granite and the shift of the textile industry to the south. The woods are dotted with old foundations, once family hearths and now stone props for wild honeysuckle and ivy. The landscape has a sadness that heightens its natural beauty; the mountains, sunlight streaming from the clouds onto the lakes and groves of birches, clear brooks lined with ferns reflecting a golden light.

Treetops has a resonance of its own. It was a place established for the founding and nurturing of a family, and a place where that family came of age. My father needed a family, and the light and fragrance of the meadows, the matchwood cottages with their old photographs, and the 1897 globe and Grandpa Watson's old books, were all artifacts of a family place.

Polly and Winter lavished charm and wit on my father. He and my mother became one of their smiled-upon couples. In the Treetops world of backbiting and favoritism, my father was treated like a prince. He slowly came to love Winter and Polly. It gave him pleasure to notice how alike he and Winter were, and seeing that a man of Winter's eccentricities could be a success gave him heart. They were both petulant, devious, competitive, and short. Because of his own father's failures, my father wrote, "I looked to other men for the force of censure, challenge, the encouragement that I needed, and was given this abundantly by Winter."

And the landscape around the lake never failed to ravish his senses. He loved climbing Cardigan or the higher mountains to the north, and sitting on the lawn with a drink and watching the evening star appear in the opalescent skies just before the final flash of green and violet sunset colors to the west.

In 1956, my father sold a story to Hollywood—his first financial windfall. In September our family—my father, myself age twelve, my brother Ben age seven, my mother four months pregnant with my brother Fred—sailed from New York to spend a year in Italy. My father was forty-four. Until then his life had revolved around four geographic poles: Treetops; his mother's little house in Quincy; Yaddo, a Saratoga Springs mansion run as a writer's colony by the magnificent Elizabeth Ames; and our house in Westchester.

🍃

In 1951 we had moved from New York City, from our apartment at 400 East 59th Street at the wrong edge of Sutton Place, out to a small cottage on the Frank Vanderlip estate in Scarborough, thirty-five miles up the Hudson River. The house, which was literally in the shadow of the white frame, ninety-room Vanderlip mansion, "Beechwood," was dark and shaped like a house built out of blocks. It had been the workshop of one of the Vanderlip children. But the forty-four-acre estate was a pastoral landscape of lawns, woods, and brooks with a flock of sheep which roamed over the meadows.

The house was rented to us through the kindness—which often seemed like charity—of the Vanderlip family and particularly Zinny Schoales, Frank Vanderlip's daughter who became a close friend of my father's. Every now and then Zinny or one of her sisters would show up at our house with a businessman from Chicago or a friend from the Cos Club who was looking for a country pied-à-terre and thought our house might be perfect. They would walk through our rooms as if we didn't exist. When the rich people had left, leaving behind the scent of expensive perfume and a few gold-ringed cigarette butts for my mother to clear away, my parents would huddle in their wake like refugees. As my father always reminded us, we had nowhere else to go. This sort of observation was often accompanied by a laugh.

My brother Ben edited *The Letters of John Cheever* and worked on the journals. He was surprised by the depth of our father's anguish. "Daddy was always hanging on like *this*," Ben says, holding up his hand in a claw. My father's desperate, tenuous hold wasn't easy for any of us, but it was hardest of all on my mother.

In all the places he lived before 1956, my father was essentially a son—sometimes troublesome, sometimes prodigal. An older generation—often an older woman—was in control, taking the responsibility and doling out the favors. In most of these places, most of the time, he used his charm and wit to great effect. He used to refer to himself at Yaddo as Little Lord Fauntleroy. We all had the enjoyment of property and luxuries that he couldn't have afforded otherwise, but we paid for that enjoyment with insecurity.

Italy changed all that for my father. It was *his* trip, made by *his* family, financed with *his* money. The elegant, shabby palazzo where we lived off the Piazza Venezia was a flat found and rented by him. Charm had nothing to do with it. It took three years after we returned from Italy for my parents to move away from the Vanderlip estate and buy their own house—but it was Italy which made that seem necessary. Being his own master at last, being able to conjure up a life in which he was the paterfamilias and we were the supplicant children, also made my father see Treetops in quite a different way.

NINE

Mountain climbing was the crucible of childhood at Treetops. At least once a week, instead of going to the beach where I loved to swim or just sit in the shallows watching the minnows nibble my toes, an obligatory climb was organized. A sadistic gleam in the eye of my father or one of my uncles at breakfast was usually the herald of a jolly four- or five-hour ordeal. The mountain of choice was Cardigan, a steep granite peak that rises to a rocky summit on the west side of Newfound Lake. The only trail that wasn't considered sissy was the Holt trail—named for the hapless Elizabeth Holt who had been blown to her death off one of its series of dizzying ledges. My first quick-march up Cardigan was at age five, and after that my presence was always required. Climbing was good for me, my parents told me. How miserably lagging behind, my head throbbing and my lungs bursting while my father and uncles bounded up the trail into the deep woods ahead, was good for me, was baffling. It felt 100 percent bad. "Just put one foot in front of the other, Susie," they would chirp, failing to take into account that their stride was three times the length of mine. I was continually afraid of being left behind or of falling backward off one of the Holt trail's precipitate ridges. The adults gave me no quarter. Once, when my sneakers raised bleeding blisters on my feet, I was encouraged to continue the climb barefoot. I didn't make it to the summit—a family disgrace. When I was twenty-one, after a winter of hard skiing, I climbed Cardigan with my father—by then a middle-aged man with a serious alcohol problem. I stayed just enough ahead so that he was panting and wheezing by the time we were halfway up the mountain. I didn't slow down, even when he had to ask me to. After that, I didn't climb another mountain for more than twenty years.

Winter and Polly wouldn't have *dreamed* of climbing Cardigan. Occasionally they'd drive with picnic hampers and blankets to a spot in the woods near a local waterfall and walk in a short way for a picnic and an icy swim. Although Winter was extremely strong and loved physical exercise himself, he did not see physical punishment as a requirement for maturity. (It was his friend Robert Hutchins who said that when he felt the urge to exercise, he lay down until it passed.) Winter and Polly didn't even walk very much. Polly liked to swim, but there were no measured distances or show-offy splashing when she did—the way there was when Uncle Bill tore off on the three-mile swim to Belle Island. Her neatly coiffed head, with a large straw hat or a tennis visor, would bob out in the water past the raft and toward Whittemore Point, and then bob back.

Winter loved ice cream and cake. Polly loved chocolates, and she didn't feel—as my parents did—that each nougat cream should be accompanied by a sharp reminder of what it was doing to my waistline and my teeth. One night at dinner, when at age twelve I had finally been allowed to eat at the grown-ups' table, I committed some breach of table manners that caused my father to explode, threatening me with banishment to the children's porch and a few other things. Polly, sitting next to me, silently reached over and squeezed my hand in a gesture of friendship and solidarity.

Each summer had its cast of characters. There was friendly Uncle Joe with his pipe and his well-turned Hotchkiss accent, Uncle Tom who never said much, and Uncle Bill, whose pretty wife, Mary, was nice to everyone—a rare trait in the family jungle of Treetops. Uncle Bill always managed to make me feel dumb.

"Point to your head and say the abbreviation for mountain," he would suggest. When he had finished chuckling at my gullibility, he'd strike again. "If cold beer is iced beer, and cold water is iced water," he'd ask, "what's cold ink?" My brothers didn't like Bill much. Once, when my father announced that he was going to the woodshed to split some kindling, my brother Fred, who was reading, declined to go with him.

"I don't like boys who don't help their fathers," Bill told Fred sternly.

"And I," replied Fred, then a senior at Andover, "don't like uncles who tell their nephews what to do." My father was delighted.

In those days, there were still loggers working Peaked Hill with handsaws and teams of draft horses.

One of the thrills of my childhood was driving up the road and over the pastures in the Studebaker with Polly at the wheel. She drove as if the car were an overland jeep. "Not passable" were not words in her vocabulary. Inevitably we got stuck, and a couple of loggers would have to be dragooned into hauling the old car back to the road with their team of horses. In Polly's world there was always someone around to help get the rich out of their scrapes.

Growing up, I wasn't much aware of the suppressed hostilities between the Whitney children and the Winternitz children—my aunts and uncles. By marrying my father, my mother had made a kind of peace with her half brothers and sisters—although she didn't mean to. My father was crazy about the Whitneys, and they liked him, too. Except for Uncle Bill, he wasn't particularly fond of the Winternitz children. Polly adored my father, and she had always favored my mother.

"Polly liked you," I remind my mother one day. Like most of our personal conversations, this one takes place on the telephone.

"It was awful."

"To be liked?"

"I was taken over to visit her, before they were married, and she was in this big four-poster bed, she always received in bed. Fortunately I said something amusing, I forget what it was.

"She was always taking me aside, or taking Bill aside, and saying how much she liked us and then saying these terrible things about our brothers and sisters," she says. Being liked by Polly wasn't something to be proud of. "She was so *mean*! I came to wish she hated me too."

Louisa visited sometimes when we were at Treetops, but her visits always had the air of being stops between two more important and glamourous destinations. Her sons, because they were older, seemed much more sophisticated and witty than the rest of us cousins. Perhaps they were. My father remembered Frank as an eight-year-old dressed in a complete miniature Brooks Brothers wardrobe. "He comes to the table in little blazers and crooked bow ties and Peale shoes," he reported in a letter to friends. "His manner is a broad imitation of Katharine Hepburn in *The Philadelphia Story.* '*Do* let's go swimming after lunch,' he exclaims, all blue eyes and crew cut. I get so nervous that I call him Fronk instead of Frank, which is his name."

The Whitneys were the same family, but they weren't the same family. The connection was as fragile as Winter's marriage to Polly—and as years went by that seemed increasingly fragile. The Whitneys talked all the time about trips to Europe, the problems with houses on the Main Line or in Greenwich, and the terrible way the Prescotts had decorated their new summer place at Northeast Harbor. My Uncle Freddy Whitney had a wonderful car with windows that went up and down automatically, a top that went up and down by machine, and another machine that sprayed jets of water on the windshield—"just like Versailles only smaller," my father wrote. It was another five years before my parents could afford any kind of car, and then it was a second-hand Dodge sedan that smelled like the inside of a discount carpet warehouse on a wet day.

For the men at Treetops who weren't content to prove their endurance by picking vegetables and plucking chickens, or their manhood by running up and down the Holt trail, there was another gladiatorial arena at Treetops—the war against marauding animals. The deer jumped over Peter Weesul's high garden fence and helped themselves to corn, as well as the baby lettuces and lima beans Winter favored. With much fanfare, my father and Uncle Bill rigged up an electric fence around the perimeter of the vegetable garden. The deer jumped over the electric fence. My father found an old rifle in the woodshed, and giving all us children a small lecture about his experience as an infantryman, he cleaned it and shot it at a few trees, which he said he hit. In the dark, things didn't go so well. Sometimes he actually blew away an ear of corn, but the deer were elusive and he was exhausted the next day. He also shot at the raccoons who got into the garden under the fence, and at the weasels who liked to raid the chicken coops—especially if someone, after an excess of postprandial libations, had forgotten to put the chickens into the chicken house before dark. He never hit a weasel—but he never hit a chicken either.

Then he bought some raccoon traps. "The first night I put them out it rained, the springs rusted and the coons left muddy foot-prints on the bait plates," he wrote in a letter. "Then I filed the traps down and have gotten them so sensitive that if I put them out before dusk they trap sparrows. This isn't much good, so today I went into town and bought . . . more traps. Mr. Follansbee at the hardware store told me to hang little pieces of mirror above the traps. 'That gits their attention,' Mr. Follansbee said. I don't know whether he was fooling or not." During the next two weeks my father managed to trap one slow-witted raccoon, and he shot and killed a porcupine that had gotten itself trapped under the washing machine.

My early summers at Treetops were often difficult. My parents' desire to put on a good show for Polly and Winter put unusual pressure on their children. But as well as protecting me, Polly also provided me with another ally, her aging children's nurse, Marie de Grasse. Marie was the loyal, genteel retainer who had seen the Whitney children through the death of their father and their mother's remarriage. A small woman who always dressed in black, Marie didn't mind telling stories by the hour in her soft voice. Taking care of children was her life.

"They made a very funny couple," my father wrote about Marie and me. "They took one another with a deadly seriousness, called one another sweet-love and other sugary nothings, and took a walk every evening after they had eaten their boiled eggs by the fire. I used to see them start off on these excursions, hand in hand, both of them equally afraid of the dark and cold, each of them sweet-loving the other. . . . Marie wore her best black and Susie wore her night-gown, her party shoes, Marie's pearls, Marie's pocket-book, and an old sweater of Marie's that trailed in the dead grass."

Many of the rituals established by my great-grandparents are still observed at Treetops. The children clean vegetables and husk corn; no one goes to the lake in the morning. For years, there was a Thursday afternoon picnic because Thursday was the cook's day off—even when there was no cook. Sunday morning the men made ice cream for Sunday lunch in the old wooden crank machine, filling it with rock salt and lining it with waxed paper to sit in the cool of the laundry until it was time for dessert. Until recently, all unmarried male visitors to Treetops slept in Bushes, the cottage furthest out in the woods above the abandoned tennis court.

Nights out there in the pine woods were dominated by naughty male activities like cigar smoking, brandy drinking, and sex talk. Steamy stories were told among the souvenirs of Uncle Bill's days at Dartmouth and in the army and Great-Uncle Harry's exploits on the polar ice cap. Dusty elk and musk-ox heads hung in the dim light next to college banners above shelves of science textbooks and an ancient victrola which played Ella Fitzgerald and Charlie Parker records. When I brought my fiancé to Treetops from college—we were both twenty years old—he was not very amused to find himself assigned to one of the lumpy twin beds in Bushes, where he was expected to swap male-bonding grunts with a crowd of my brothers and cousins.

At Treetops, the morning is for work—shopping or cleaning vegetables or mowing lawns. A cook still dominates the big kitchen—even though the cook is sometimes my mother. Food is still served in willowware dishes on the big table on the porch. The keys are still kept in the ice bucket. There are elaborate rules for opening and closing each cottage. Fuses are loosened, newspapers are laid neatly across each bed, boxes of rat poison are put out for the winter—at least once a decade a dog or child has to be rushed to the hospital for a stomach pumping after eating one of these boxes. Ropes are hung from the bathtub faucets so that mice won't get trapped there to die. The hot water is turned off, pillows are stored in bureau drawers, and the blankets are returned to a chest in the laundry behind Apple.

T E N

"I HAVE MY TROUBLES," my father wrote from Treetops to his friend John Weaver in July of 1947, when I was almost four years old.

Mrs. Fitch French, who does my wash, has a middle-aged and crippled cat she wants Susie to have. Susie wants the cat. I don't want Susie to have the cat so on Sunday I bought three rabbits; one for Susie and one each for Irene and Jackie, the cook's children. This cost four dollars. Then I brought the rabbits home. I put them in an old duck pen where I thought they would be comfortable. . . . The next evening when Susie went to [the pen] to feed her bunny she found that he was dead. She screamed. She cried. She was inconsolable. I buried the rabbit at the head of the garden while the gardener stood beside me and told me I was wasting my time. I should throw the rabbit into the woods for the skunks, he said. He is a communist and is so steeled against bourgeois sentimentality that he hasn't even given his horse a name. I then went to the duck pen to investigate the cause of the bunny's death and found some poison there, left for the rats by "Guts" Winternitz, my father-in-law. This poison was manufactured by the Chemical Warfare Branch of the United States Army to be fed, presumably, to Russians. All of the rabbits tasted the poison but only one of them died. Do you think this is a threat to our national security? Do you think there ought to be a shake-up in chemical warfare? . . . there's a lot of talk about filling the void in Susie's life with Mrs. Fitch French's crippled cat.

By the early 1950s my parents' lives had settled into a relatively stable postwar routine. They had two children, they had moved to the little house on the Vanderlip estate, and my father paid the bills by writing short stories, usually for *The New Yorker*. Since the magazine didn't pay much—often as little as $300 for a story—he had to write a lot of them. We went to Treetops every summer during those years, and my father used Treetops and my mother's family as the subtext for some of the stories.

In "The Day the Pig Fell into the Well," he wrote a story about a family's relationship to its summer place. The story shows a family growing up in the place—Whitebeach Camp—during and after World War II, and it returns again and again to the leitmotiv of the stories the family tells about itself. Another example of the way my father took facts, his own fears, and a few characters, and wove them into a thoroughly transcendent story is "The Summer Farmer," which he wrote from the incident of the poisoned rabbits—the same incident that made such a funny letter to John Weaver.

What's comic in the letter takes on a tone of menace and foreboding in the short story. The communist farmer, a man like Peter Weesul, becomes sinister. In the story he is an immigrant named Kasiak whose disdain for capitalism is equaled by his disdain for Paul Hollis, a gentleman farmer who commutes on weekends from a city job to join his wife and two children. In the story, the children's crying is no joke. "He heard that noise that he dreaded above all others—his innocent and gentle children screaming in pain." Hollis is relieved to find that they are only crying over dead rabbits, but alarmed to find the cause—"mortal poison" that was used to kill the rats. He confronts the surly Kasiak, vaguely suspecting him of wanting to harm not just the rabbits, but his children. He yells at the farmer and accuses him, but gets no answer. In a rage ignited by his own fears, Hollis threatens Kasiak, and then pushes him down, so that the man sprawls in the dirt. Later Hollis' wife asks if the rabbits were poisoned. When he says yes, she explains that she put the poison out. "I never thought we'd use that house again, and I wanted to keep the rats out of it. I forgot. . . . I completely forgot."

In another story, "The Common Day," the elusive coons made it into the pages of *The New Yorker*. "As he approached the corn patch, he could hear a wild, thin crying. Then the animal, whatever it was, began to pound the dirt. The stroke was strong, as regular as a heartbeat." Jim, the protagonist, reaches the trapped raccoon and shoots it. As he walks toward the toolhouse with the trap and limp carcass, a refined old woman servant calls to him from a field where she is standing with a precious little girl—his niece Carlotta.

" 'Where's the coon?' Carlotta asked.

" 'The coon's gone on a long, long journey, dear,' Agnes said. 'Come now, come along, sweet. . . .' They turned and started back toward the house, warning one another of the sticks and ditches and other perils of the country. Their conversation was filled with diminutives, timidity, and vagueness. He wanted to help them, he wanted urgently to help them, he wanted to offer them his light, but they reached the house without his help and he heard the back door close on their voices."

Peter Weesul appears in many of the stories about Treetops. Peter had immigrated from Latvia to Boston, where he'd worked cutting bricks in an ice cream factory. But he was a farmer, and when he had saved some money in the New World, he and his wife and daughter traveled north to find some land they could farm for themselves. Peter was a boyish, angular man, whose sleeves and pant legs were always a little short. He wore high-top sneakers. His face was sunburned up to a line across his forehead where his cap sat. When he doffed it, to wipe the sweat away with a red bandanna, a stripe of pale flesh lay below his sandy-colored hair. He fascinated my father with his quiet resentment of the rich (which my father shared, but did not dare express because he also loved the rich), his easygoing and perfect communication with the soil and growing things, and his political beliefs. In his fiction, my father used Peter Weesul's politics as a symbol. In story after story, the immigrant farmer mocks the summer farmer and talks back to the lady of the house, who doesn't understand her own gar-

dens. He is the man who watches and judges. The Winternitzes and the Whitneys came and went at Treetops, using
nature's gifts for their own pleasure. Peter Weesul was always
there.

At first, in my father's early stories, Peter is a kind of noble
savage. Then, in "The Summer Farmer," he becomes a menac-
ing and somehow judging force. Later, in "How Dr. Wareham
Kept His Servants," the farmer is blackmailed into servitude by
a cruel, calculating employer, who threatens to expose his communist past.

When I was a girl, Peter lived in the brown farmhouse with
his deaf daughter, Ella. Behind the pretty farmhouse was a
rich, open pasture, one of the most beautiful curves of hillside
in New Hampshire, with wide open views of the lake. Peter
planted a row of small fir trees between the top of his pasture
and the hill that drops steeply away from the Stone House. By
the time my grandfather died, these fir trees—fast-growing
white pine—had grown up to a thick wall completely obscur-
ing the views of the lake from the Stone House. My mother calls
this fir grove Peter Weesul's revenge.

When I was a child, I was told that our family had once
owned the entire hillside as far up as the eye could see and as
far down as the glassy waters of the lake. Other people who
lived on the hill had come by their property through our
generosity. The little red house at the top and the white saltbox at the end of an avenue of maples had been given to
doctors who came to look after my grandmother. The red
farmhouse above us and the brown one below had been given
to the two Peters. This myth about family magnanimity be-

came another apocryphal tale about the resentment of Peter Weesul and the encroachment of the world on our family stronghold.

When Peter Weesul died, his daughter Ella was afraid to live on alone in the farmhouse. Charlie Greenwood, a local school-teacher whose brother is the town plumber, bought the Weesul land for a few thousand dollars in return for providing Ella with some company and an apartment in town. Once Ella died, Charlie took title. He bulldozed the beautiful curve of Peter's pasture and, right at the top, built a bright blue ranch house with a deck. He turned Peter's old farmhouse into apartments. He loves to drop into Treetops to remind us of how close to our houses his property line runs and to suggest that he has big plans for building.

Of course the family mythology is wrong. The building on the hill is not a backfire of my grandfather's generosity, but normal growth. Watson bought fifty acres, not the whole hillside—when he bought it, he wasn't a rich man anymore. Both Peter Weesul and Pete Charron were here before we began to build.

In the 1850s the hill was a busy place, with most of the woods cleared for farming and six or seven farmhouses along the dirt road that runs along the brook as it cascades to the lake. In Grandpa Watson's time, the farmers were gone, but there were still a few summer houses for people from Boston in the days when mountain air was thought to be beneficial to health. When I was growing up, the hill was deserted. Two of the farmhouses were falling down, one was a cellar hole, and the wall of Pete Charron's barn had crumbled, so that I could see where he had hung his jacket on a hook near the hayloft earlier on the day that he died in the woods, probably of a heart attack. The only person who lived above us was an old hermit in a tar paper shack who spent the winter months in the Bristol jail. Now the hill is busier than ever. New Hampshire is one of the richest and fastest growing states in the Union. There are seven new houses above us, and the road, once a narrow dirt track, has been graded and paved.

Another family story, which contradicts the story about my grandfather's magnanimity to Peter Weesul (contradiction is rarely a drawback in family stories), tells how Peter came to Newfound Lake looking for land to farm. To the real-estate agent's amazement, when she drove Peter up to the brown farmhouse, he didn't go inside. Instead he walked up into the pasture and sifted the soil through his fingers, smelling it and fingering it as if it were a precious metal. He bought the land. No one farms it now.

The last time I saw Peter alive was in 1967. I was spending a week in May at the Stone House, and three times a day Peter came in through the kitchen and stoked the old wood-burning furnace below the living room floor so that we would be warm. I never saw him, only at dawn I could hear the thump of his sneakers as he let himself into the kitchen and walked down the hollow frame stairs to the cellar. When I got home from skiing at night, a stream of smoke would be curling out of the chimney. Before I left Treetops that winter, I went to visit Peter in his farmhouse—something I had never done before. He came out of the brown shingle house with his daughter Ella standing frightened behind him in the shadow of the doorway. I had never touched Peter, but on the pathway of his house that morning, we embraced. We both knew he was dying. He was

wearing his overalls and those high-top sneakers. He smelled
of the earth.

As my mother and Winter got older, my father began to see
Treetops in a different light. Every family exerts its own mag-
netic force, and my father began to notice how powerful it was
for my mother. Slowly, Winter's increasing influence started to
appear as a malignant power on my mother and on the chemistry of our family.

As my father became more successful in the 1950s, Winter's
success was less impressive. Polly and Winter began to nag
each other and to complain about each other to my father—or
anyone who would listen. At the same time my parents started
quarreling with each other more often. There were more angry
silences, and fewer affectionate reconciliations.

My father anchored his sanity with the weight of his family.
His fears for us were always exaggerated, and at Treetops they
got worse. There, his wife was under an alien influence and his
children were subject to perils he could not control. At Treetops, my father was no longer the man of the family—Winter
was—and eventually this became intolerable.

As the harmony between my parents deteriorated, and Winter's hold over my mother tightened, my father brooded. As
always, his sulk was mythic in dimension. Sometimes he
thought he was a male Demeter, condemned to share his beloved Persephone with Hades, the evil king of the underworld,
and forced to watch in anguish as she was returned to his
powerful influence for a part of each year. Other times he was
Orpheus, armed only with his lyre, vainly trying to lead his

Eurydice out of the realm of the underworld. In either scenario, Winter didn't have a very good part.

In a 1960s short story, one of three titled "Metamorphoses," my father wrote about Orville Betman, a man who falls in love with his wife on a Fifth Avenue bus. "The instant he saw her he felt a singular attraction or passion that he had never felt before and would never, as it happened, feel again."

Betman finds out the woman's name is Victoria Heatherstone. She's a Vassar graduate who lives with, and for, her cranky, invalid father, a Trollope scholar. She laughs at Betman's proposal of marriage; she says she can't leave her father. Providentially, the aging tyrant has a stroke and moves to a house he owns on an island in a remote lake. With the new arrangement, Victoria stays with her father during the summer, three months a year. The other nine months she is blissfully married to Betman. But Betman is still jealous, and one summer he drives to the remote lake to reclaim his wife. She abandons her father and leaves with her husband, but she is killed in an automobile accident on the way back to New York.

My mother and her sister Buff were the two children at Treetops the day Winter left. My father had stopped his annual visits a few years before. Polly had stormed out after a fight, leaving a cloud of dust as she tore down the driveway. "If you want me, you can reach me care of Thomas Cook and Sons," she said. My mother and Buff drove down the familiar dirt road to the Stone House to get their father and take him to Hanover, an hour west of Bristol; he had an appointment at the hospital there.

"Let's have a dish of ice cream before we go," he said. He

loved sweets. It was a beautiful day at the end of August in 1959, and sunlight, filtered through the maple trees, danced on the paneled walls of the house and on the old oriental rug. But his daughters were worried about the time, and so Winter got in the car without his ice cream and was driven off, down the driveway, past the big copper beech and the lily pond and his own high bush blueberries and Polly's cutting garden in the golden afternoon. Winter died in October.

By the time of his death, there was nothing left of his friendship with my father except disappointment. Their closeness, based on Winter's generosity and my father's admiration of his eccentric success, and eased by large amounts of gin, had disintegrated into anger and confusion.

My father had begun to feel he couldn't work at Treetops. He would set up his typewriter in Winter's old laboratory, but just as he'd get going, the old man would appear to clip the flowers under his window and start a conversation through the screen.

My father, who could be supremely, cruelly sarcastic, moody, and divisive, began to notice these qualities more and more in his father-in-law. Winter was irascible, he complained. Winter brutalized relationships. Winter's was the "perfect Stalinist intelligence," he wrote, in its devotion only to results.

More and more often my father would accompany us to Treetops for a few days of backgammon and heavy drinking and one climb up Cardigan and then head back to New York City where he holed up in a cheap hotel and tried to work. The place he had once thought was his personal paradise had come to seem like a bad Restoration comedy. Winter's wit was nothing but nastiness. Polly's class was nothing more than name dropping. Everyone was scheming and whispering, gossiping about and plotting against everyone else.

Polly and Winter, now in their seventies, were hurt and bewildered by my father's change of heart. They became demanding, querulous, and nostalgic—all things he hated.

"Since my relationships with Mary have not been good," he wrote in his journals, "I have thought of her parents with less and less friendliness, less and less love." At a dinner party at Janie Whitney Hotchkiss' house, Polly and Winter infuriated him. He felt that Winter was emotionally dishonest. "Pretending to suffer from emotional indigestion when he is stuffed with Polish ham, . . . and the old man's reluctance to grant anyone their independence. . . . I have less and less patience with this. . . . I love these good people, but how much can I love them if they seem to threaten my happiness and the happiness of my sons and my daughter and it seems as if they could bring great sorrow down onto us all," he wrote.

The heart of the change was a fierce, unacknowledged struggle in which my father set himself up to try and overpower the past. When my parents were first married, they had a palpable sense of relief in each other's presence. My mother thought that my father had saved her from the cruelties of her childhood; he thought she had rescued him from the sordidness of his own. My father told me that when they were young, my mother's love for him had enabled her to see that Winter—who had caused her so much pain—was nothing but an old fool. Armed with my father's love, she could laugh at Winter's attempts to draw her back into the web of childhood patterns.

But as the years wore on, the past reasserted itself. Winter was able to disconcert my mother, or please her, and my father was helpless again. He had less and less effect on her. Winter's generosity made her glow; his cruelty cut her to the bone. My father's similarities to Winter—which had once been so delightful—were now deeply disturbing and had to be disowned. Could he possibly be as negative, sarcastic, and quixotic as this old man? Winter's rich, complex personality, his alternate openness and meanness, was a mirror in which my father was less and less pleased to see his own face.

My mother took her father's side. It had been twenty years since she introduced the shy young writer to her overbearing and successful father. Now that the writer was successful and Winter was dying, everything seemed different. Her own father, wounded by a man who had wounded her so much, was impossible to resist. When he lay dying in a hospital in Hanover that fall, my mother says, Winter asked again and again to see my father, to hear from my father. My father refused. He thought the old man was faking. He resented the way Winter's death took all my mother's attention. He wouldn't go. My mother says that she never forgave him for that.

❦

Winter's funeral in New Haven was an austere, grim occasion. A light rain fell on the Winternitz and Whitney mourners standing around the open grave at the cemetery. Bill was working at a hospital in England and didn't come back. Buff was in òne of her manic moods and wouldn't stop talking about Winter's will. Tom and Jane were somber, my mother upset and silent.

"I have simmered down thoroughly," she wrote to her

brother Bill in England a month after the ceremony. "I think it is just another pathetic fallacy to wish a person more peace and contentment at the end of his life, because, as things are, he is more likely to have less. Perhaps that's part of death. Having been so close to it I felt terribly frustrated and wound up."

After the funeral the Whitneys went off to a small reception at the Lawn Club and the Winternitzes went home.

ELEVEN

When Tolstoy wrote that all happy families are alike, what he meant was that there are no happy families. The family is as confining as it is nurturing. Our need for this community keeps us in a cage of other people's desires and expectations; some of us spend our lives peering out through the bars at what seems to be a larger world. Every family has its own cast of characters—the pretty and the plain, the weak and the strong, the bright and the dull, the cop and the rebel. Family members each play a role, which is sometimes so inalterable that they seem to be reading from a script. In the world outside the family, they have the freedom to change and to establish who they are through actions. At home, they will always be the character they were as a child within the family context. No matter what their successes, members of their family will forever see them reliving the failures of their youth.

My Uncle Bill, the youngest, will always be the baby in his family, although he's now a man in his seventies. He's a distinguished doctor, but his sisters still fuss over his health. For years he taught at Yale Medical School, then he moved to the new medical school at the University of Kentucky in Lexington. Now he is a professor and chief of Internal Medicine at the University of Alabama in Tuscaloosa. He lives in a house at the edge of a thick pine grove on a lake in the Alabama woods. The surrounding land is owned by a paper tycoon who likes to be called Captain. Naval cannons and anchors mark the intersections, and the streets are called Commodore Drive and Admiral Way although they're five hundred miles from the gulf. Winter's desk from his office at Yale, the desk that used to look, to young medical school applicants, like the endlessly high wall of an armed fortress, is now Bill's desk for work he brings home. Bill was always the athletic son, the one who would insist on climbing Cardigan in a snowstorm or swimming across the lake before breakfast. He has taken over the management of Treetops in the past decade, hiring a competent caretaker, turning over the mortgage, and assessing family members for improvements. But he has to watch it now. He has grandchildren. He worries about his cholesterol—something they hadn't even discovered back in those Treetops summers when he watched the Whitney boys pick on his sisters, or when he was a young medical student who went out with all the pretty nurses.

Buff was always the smart sister, even when she was institutionalized and spent her days making baskets for therapy. "I never bothered to remember anything," her sister Jane told me. "Buff had a wonderful memory and I counted on her to remember everything for me."

Jane was the little mother. She was bossy enough to take over when her mother and then her older sister Buff both faltered. She became Winter's favorite, and she lived with him and Polly at 210 Prospect Street while she was getting a graduate degree. My father used to say that this experience was so searing that after that she never wanted to see him again. My mother says it was Polly whom Jane never wanted to see again. At any rate, she and her children seldom came to Treetops. They were not at the Christmas celebrations I remember as a child in New Haven. Although they lived near us in the New York suburbs, we never saw them as I was growing up.

My Uncle Tom looks so much like his father that when I see him now, wearing socks and shoes and Bermuda shorts as he walks past the garage at Treetops or across the oval lawn, I think I'm seeing a ghost. But it is not Winter, come back to examine his sheds and gardens—he would surely find them wanting—it is his son. Later, when I go down to the Stone House where Tom and his wife Betty are staying, I find them blithely watching a television they have brought in the sacred precincts of Winter's old study. His portrait glares angrily, and helplessly, down from the paneled wall.

Tom was always the family blunderer. His white lies and petty thefts—normal limit-testing for a kid—were cast in bronze and hung on him like a leper's bells. He was too stupid, I was always told, to go into medicine, too stupid for anything but a mediocre academic career arranged through his father's friends—first at Loomis School and then at the University of Chicago—leading to a sinecure at Bell Labs, the family business. Tom became an electrical engineer, and we all laughed at his fishing trips into Newfound Lake in a rowboat bristling with sonar equipment and antennae. He rarely caught anything, while his adept brother Bill could haul them in from the shore using a worm and a rusty hook.

But on Tom's resume, on file at Bell Labs, I notice two Harvard degrees—an M.A. and a Ph.D.

"Oh, I think Betty helped him with that, *she's* very smart you know," my mother explained when I asked her about them. "Tom could never get anything quite right." It's not that my mother doesn't love and respect her brother Tom—I think she does. It's just that her hold on things still depends a little on the accuracy of her family's mythology. These old stories about who she is and who they are are the shaky foundation on which her view of the world is built. If they shift, anything can shift.

Most of Tom's records at Bell Labs are classified. The rest were kept in a locked archive until a few years ago, when a team of government agents spent a year at Bell Labs shredding almost everything in it. The researchers at Bell Labs can't tell me much. They know that Tom was on Kwajalein Island in the Pacific during a project in which U.S. missiles were tested, and that he was executive director of the team sent to Iran to establish a communications system for the shah. Tom has been working in top secret military communications all these years.

But within the family, Tom still obliges by acting the dunce. Tom's refusal to go into medicine—the field that his father regarded as the only proper study of mankind—so enraged Winter that the scars of his fury still show. "When he had no use for you, that was *it*," Tom remembers. "Conversation was no longer necessary."

Tom is certainly the nicest of the five siblings. Maybe he didn't have to prove anything. Maybe he had nothing to lose.

"They tell me you're writing something I won't like," he says to me, smiling. "I don't care, I hope you write whatever you want and good luck! I figure I won't be around many years to read it anyway." Of all my aunts and uncles, Tom is the only one who has ever said a word about my writing. He took a moment to tell me how much he liked my first novel. Later I found the copy he'd read with his place marked at page 40. That made his compliment even more valuable.

Tom and Bill and their sisters now have the advantage of age. They have seen the world, but when they are at Treetops, it *is* their world. Tom used to drive eight hours from his office in New Jersey at Bell Labs, jump out of the car, and methodically mow all the Treetops grass—still dressed in his regulation dark suit, white shirt, black tie, and tie shoes. When Bill is at Treetops he paints and chops wood and makes lists of chores. My mother and her brothers cook and mow, chop and pick, patch and paint as if Winter's deep voice were still barking orders somewhere above them. They have their own children and grandchildren now, but at Treetops they are still children. They labor to soothe the dead in a place where the dead are still very much alive.

After Winter's death, my mother grew into a late-blossoming confidence and talent which lasted more than a decade. By the 1960s, then, her children were mostly grown—I was at college and Ben was at boarding school. My father had won a measure of financial security, and they had bought and moved into their own glorious house in Ossining, a few miles north of the Vanderlip estate.

Susan Cheever

For the first time in thirty years my mother took a job—teaching English three days a week at nearby Briarcliff Junior College, an institution famous more for the good looks of its students than for academic excellence. The Briarcliff girls adored my mother. Their good looks seemed to rub off on her. She was also, as it turned out, a superb teacher. She took yoga classes and began to dress as elegantly as her students, emerging as a stunningly attractive woman. She went to a psychiatrist and bought herself a new family car.

My mother's transformation was the result of multiple forces, but it was a dramatic proof of what a salaried job can do for a woman's self-esteem. For once, she was valued for what she did with her mind and her imagination, instead of at the stove or the ironing board. Children are always ambivalent; her students gave her simple admiration and uncomplicated gratitude. She became a combination idol and den mother for the daughters of the rich who had been sent to Briarcliff, and she also developed intense friendships with some other members of the college English department—her first friendships outside her marriage in more than twenty years.

But my mother's new strength was profoundly threatening for my father. For a lot of reasons, his view of sexual roles was both rigid and old-fashioned. Women should be submissive and pretty, and men should be strong and provide for their wives and families. He was upset if he found one of his sons cooking or sweeping. "That's women's work" was a family phrase which for my father was less than half a joke.

My father was bisexual. My mother never acknowledged this but it turns out she knew it. With his intense needs and expectations about women and his lust for men, my father had plenty of confusion to struggle with.

There was also the past. When his mother had abandoned her "feminine" role to take a job and support the family, the family had disintegrated. It was my grandfather's drinking and inability to find a job that drove my grandmother to work for money; in *my* father's mind this cause and effect had always been reversed. He never forgave his mother for usurping what he saw as his father's role, and he never forgave her for not being the attentive, constant, housebound mother he dreamed about.

By the late sixties, my parents' house had become a full-fledged sexual battleground. As my father drank more, my mother's increasing satisfaction outside their home became a constant thorn. He told anyone who would listen that her income actually impoverished the family by putting us in a higher tax bracket. He continually pointed out how silly it was for her—the wife of a great writer—to be teaching writing to a bunch of sexy bubbleheads. He wrote story after story about the disastrous effects of women abandoning their household roles. In "The Geometry of Love" a husband dies of his wife's selfishness. In "An Educated American Woman" a little boy dies because of his mother's defection from the hearth.

Each spring, as my mother began to plan her annual trip to Treetops, the war escalated. Her two or three weeks in New Hampshire were taken by my father as a complete, unequivocal abandonment. Although he had often left Treetops himself to spend time alone in New York, now he used every possible ruse to avoid being left alone. He complained bitterly and constantly. He made it sound as if her time at Treetops was a year. Often, he got sick as the date of her departure approached. He threw full-scale tantrums.

My mother went anyway. She cooked and froze two weeks of meals for him, paid the cleaning lady in advance, lined up as many dinners with friends as she could manage, packed up her station wagon with my brother Fred and the dogs, and took off. Usually within a few days my father had broken the oven and filled the sink with dirty dishes. Once I dropped in on him when my mother had been gone a few days and found him heating a package of frozen macaroni and cheese. The oven wasn't broken yet, but my father refused to read the instructions on the macaroni and cheese box. He had no idea how long or at what temperature to bake it. As a result, he took it out of the oven every ten minutes or so and scraped the cooked part onto a plate, eating it in pathetic increments.

Because of the disruption of my mother's annual trip to Treetops, my father said, he was unable to work for months. When he did write, he produced bitter stories like "Marito in Città" about forlorn men in empty houses, neglected by their wives and children, who had larked off to their vacation in the mountains. "He fried himself some eggs, but he found that he couldn't eat them," writes the narrator in "Marito," when his wife and children have gone. "He made an Old-Fashioned cocktail with particular care and drank it. Then he returned to the eggs, but he still found them revolting. He drank another cocktail and approached the eggs from a different direction, but they were still repulsive."

There were battles about sex, but there were also many skirmishes about food. In the face of my mother's absence, my father behaved as if he might literally starve to death. Instead, he spent a lot of time in local restaurants drinking too much and blamed it on my mother, and he found other women to cook for him—women who sometimes slept with him, too—and this was also my mother's fault. But my mother did not change course. Instead, she started writing poetry, and she had a brief, wrenching and passionate affair with another writer.

Although my mother's transformation was not as dramatic later as it was during the sixties, she never lost the strength and sense of humor she gained during those years.

In the winter of 1974, between two almost fatal bouts of alcoholic heart disease, my father—who was broke again—taught a semester at the Iowa Writers' Workshop at the University of Iowa. He came back bursting with stories about his love affair with N. N. loved him totally, passionately, he boasted. N. wrote him two or three love letters a day. Often his tales about N. were told in my mother's kitchen or at the dining room table over a meal she prepared.

In the spring, when my mother began making plans for her weeks in New Hampshire, my father resumed his bitter complaints about her departure. N. was still writing him love letters, but that didn't seem to make any difference. "Your *mother*," my father would say with an angry twist to his voice, "will not be here this summer." Any mention of the future brought a lament. "She prefers the company of her brothers and sisters," he would say.

But this time, instead of trying to compensate for her absence, cooking two weeks' worth of meals and steeling herself against the inevitable indictment for failure to be a proper wife, my mother picked up the telephone and called N. She was going away for a few weeks in August, she explained to N., but

John didn't like to be left alone. She asked if N. would consider moving into the house and taking care of him while she was gone. N. accepted with delight. My father was checkmated. He quickly ended his relationship with the young girl—there were a few tearful telephone calls for my father and then nothing—but it was too late to salvage anyone's pity, even his own. My mother had called his bluff, and his complaints about her time in New Hampshire lost their weight. No one ever took them seriously again.

TWELVE

My PARENTS BUILT a marriage that survived more than forty years of secrets and publicity, anger and passion, hard times and wild successes. Sometimes their marriage was a triumph; sometimes it seemed more like a testimony to the endurance of human bondage. My father needed the marriage—my mother kept it together. She had met and married my father under mind-altering pressures when she was too young to imagine the course her life would take. My father idealized her and often blamed her for falling short of his female fantasy—a woman who was strong, but gentle enough not to remind anyone that she was strong. A woman, as he once wrote, who would laughingly let a man win at tennis even if she could play better. Whatever their miseries with each other—and they were many and loudly expressed—my parents created a family intensely and proudly bound. Most of the time it was fun to be with them; some of the time they were magic.

As soon as he made enough money to stop worrying about

next month's rent, my father began to take all of us—and anyone else who wanted to come along—on wonderful trips. Traveling—where his generosity could have full rein but his world was insulated from outside disruptions—my father was at his funny, charming best, and my mother responded to that. First, we went to Italy. Then he took us all to the Caribbean, where he befriended an ex-spy who ran a posh resort on the coast of Curaçao. We swam along the continental shelf, bought watches in the duty-free shops at Willemstad, and signed for many, many gin and tonics. He took my mother and my brother Fred to Italy to interview Sophia Loren for a magazine. Fred spent one prep school vacation raising hell in Russia with my father and his pal Yevgeny Yevtushenko. Ben went with him to Bulgaria and got a Black Sea suntan. We all went to Mallorca and called on Robert Graves. The day in 1979 my father won the Pulitzer Prize for his collected stories, he had somehow arranged it so that we were all—including one of the dogs—staying at his favorite hotel, the Boston Ritz on Commonwealth Avenue. Heads turned when we walked, as a family, into the great dining room with its windows looking out on the Public Gardens, and the chef produced a spectacular flaming Baked Alaska. At times like this my mother struck a perfect balance between being a famous writer's wife and being an intelligent woman with her own resources. He was the center of attention, but she knew how much she had contributed to his success.

When my parents bought their house in Ossining in 1961, our sense of family intensified. Named "Afterwhiles," it's a graceful house with terraces, lawns, a pine woods, and a brook running down the hill into a series of ponds. My father called it

"Meanwhiles"; my mother titled it "The Grecian Earn." In creating our immediate family—and its myth—my parents succeeded in a superb collaboration. Although there was often friction between us siblings or between us and one or the other parent, as a unit we were loyal, closely knit and passionately attached to our sense of this group of five. When my father told my brother on a playing field once to "remember that you are a Cheever," he wasn't talking about ancestry, but rather about a family where failure was often mixed with success, where literate intelligence was a bottom line, where pain was expressed as humor and where any pretension or self-promotion was fair game for the sharp wits of the other family members. When my father got good reviews, we all used the sappiest lines to tease him. When he had the book jacket of my mother's book of poetry framed, she was justifiably furious. Medals or prizes were tossed into drawers and forgotten.

My father was the soloist, the virtuoso, and my mother was the orchestra. At the house in Ossining in the 1960s and 1970s when—most of the time—financial pressures were eased and the children had all become conversationally adept adults, they were in top form. All kinds of people were entertained, and all were treated alike whether it was Brooke Astor for lunch or a college friend of Ben's for dinner. My mother was a superb cook, who could also bring the house down with an acerbic comment as she passed the cheese board. She furnished the house with comfortable old-fashioned furniture and a few antiques. When we children dropped in for lunch we might run into Alan Moorehead doing his impersonation of the Australian Kudzu bird—and endangering the lamps—Brendan Behan explaining his interest in what he called "the farney" (sex), or the Updikes or Philip Roth talking with my mother in the kitchen about the late work of William Carlos Williams.

My parents had had lean years, and the house in Ossining was alive with their infectious and generous enjoyment of success. One Christmas when my Volkswagen wouldn't start, we all piled into the car and drove down to Croton to buy a new one before lunch. Later, when I wanted to use it to drive to Bucks County and spend the weekend with a male friend, my parents balked. It was Ralph Ellison, who happened to be there for lunch, who persuaded them that, at age twenty, I was old enough to take care of myself. In 1969, for no reason at all, they threw a grand party for me and my first husband, a gala with a tent and dancing and people getting drunk and dogs scrounging for scraps and lives being changed. My mother and I shopped for the dress and the caterer. Hundreds of guests in formal clothes walked down across the lawns to the tent and people are still talking about it.

In fact, the family house was so comforting and so much fun that it took us children a while to start our own families. My husband and I lived within five miles; my brother Ben moved to a house nearby. Fred was often home, even after he went off to Andover. None of us had children. Then, in the year my father died, we all got married—Ben and I for the second time, Fred for the first. In the years since my father's last illness we've had four children between us. This results in a lot of tired older parents running around after toddlers at family gatherings.

My parents became better friends during these years, partly because they each developed a life outside the marriage. For my mother there were friendships with other teachers and students. It was a time when she was at her most beautiful and her

Shelling peas on the oval lawn at Treetops: (left to right) Buff, Mary Winternitz, William Welch Winternitz (Bill), Esther Watson, Janie Hotchkiss, and
Steven Whitney.

ABOVE: Susan (left) and Ben Cheever (in striped shirt) with cousins at Treetops.

LEFT: Elizabeth Winternitz (Buff).

RIGHT: Mary and her sister Buff.

BELOW: Winter and Mary at Prospect Street.

(left to right adults): Mary, Elizabeth Austin Winternitz (Betty), Mary Prymak Winternitz, Bill, Buff, and children in front of Apple.

LEFT: Mary and Bill mountain climbing with dogs.

BELOW: Mary, Bill, and Jane Winternitz.

John Cheever's funeral in Norwell, Massachusetts: Mary and Susan (front), family members, John Updike (left).

LEFT: Susan (pregnant with Sarah) and Federico Cheever (Fred) in Ossining.

BELOW: Susan and baby Sarah.

ABOVE: Sarah's christening at Treetops: the Rev. Frank Griswold, Susan holding Sarah, Patricia and Charles Gaines (friends), Mary, Eliza, and Phoebe Griswold.

BELOW: Sarah at the Stone House, Summer 1983.

most self-contained. My parents seemed to have let go of one another in a way which allowed them to live in relative harmony.

My father's life outside the marriage was somewhat less decorous than my mother's. In the late 1960s when he began having an affair with Hope Lange, he started talking about his mistresses and sexual conquests to anyone who would listen. My mother's discretion, and her fierce protectiveness toward any part of her life which was hers and hers alone, saved our family at this point. We were all able to laugh at my father, my mother was laughing at him after all, and this kept us together under strains which might have pulled apart another kind of household. Because of this, we children were sympathetic to my mother and angry at my father. My mother kept her private life private; my father's private life was as embarrassingly public as he could make it. He was covering his tracks, of course. What *he* was keeping private were his affairs with men. Maybe it was just a matter of style. My mother was obviously caught in the ancient feminine struggle between self and family. My father was just telling stories.

It was a few years later that my mother and I went to the movies in Ossining at the new theater in the Arcadian Shopping Center—named for the greenhouses and gardens that filled the land as I was growing up. Without actually planning it, we ended up seeing *Death Wish*, a movie that begins when the hero's wife is murdered by a pack of mocking, angry black kids armed with a can of red spray paint. The wife was played by Hope Lange. My mother and I sat silently and watched as Hope (in a flashback) cavorted charmingly on a beach, and we watched without comment as she was beaten to death in her own living room.

After my father died I asked Hope Lange about him; I asked her how serious she thought their affair had been.

"How serious could it be?" she asked. "He always had to take the 5:20 train home."

PART THREE

THIRTEEN

In 1984 I gave a reading from *Home Before Dark*, a biographical memoir about my father, at Books & Co., a bookstore on Madison Avenue. I invited my mother to introduce me, and she surprised me by saying yes. In her introduction, she talked about the questions people ask her in her role as the wife of a writer and the mother of a writer. Her questions were as revealing as her answers.

The first question she talked about was "What's it like not to have any secrets?" She stood at the shaky podium at the front of a long room on the second floor of the store, where the audience sat on folding chairs. As she proceeded, the people in the front rows looked at each other for confirmation of what they were hearing. Most people expect boring, predictable encomiums when parents get up to talk about their children in public. My mother is not predictable. She dodged the first question, saying that she still did have secrets, and went on to the second.

"Did you always know that your daughter was capable of

such an accomplishment?" This was a tough question since—although she had read *Home Before Dark* in manuscript a year before it was published, and although I had made the dozens of changes she suggested—my mother had recently been quoted in the press as saying that the book was inaccurate and that she wished I hadn't written it. Typically for our family, she had used a public medium to tell me something she had been reluctant to tell me in private. This was a sore point between us; a sore point that, of course, neither of us mentioned.

"In the tradition of absolute candor which has been recently established for our family, I admit that I did not always know," she answered. By this time, some of the audience were in shock. "I rather hoped the children would be scientists of some sort," she went on. "Write if you must, I would tell them, but get some useful scientific training so that you can always make a living." This was strange advice from the wife of a man who had supported his family with the earnings from his writings for forty years. "There was not much encouragement," she concluded. "Although there was one heady season when Susie got an A in Geometry, this was as far as she went toward becoming the lab technician I urged her to be."

Some people in the audience thought she was joking. Actually, she was joking. What passes for friendly joking in my family often seems like a frontal assault to other people. Others in the audience were taken aback by her aloofness from my work. But that remoteness was no aberration—remoteness is a defining characteristic of my mother's personality. It's a protective distance she has developed in reaction to the stresses of her life, embodied first in her parents and siblings and then in her husband and children.

There are some stories about my mother and her bizarre, disorienting response to her children's needs. Direct answers are difficult for her, reassurance is usually not her style. "I hope I won't always be this lonely," I would sigh, when I was an adolescent. "Have a piece of this nice cheese!" my mother would say, or "Oh, Susie, could you let the dogs in?"

Another time my mother came to hear me speak on a panel at the Roosevelt Hotel with Jill Robinson, the novelist and daughter of playwright and screenwriter Dore Schary. Jill reverently described how her father had helped her with her first book, lovingly editing and encouraging her, and urging her on when she flagged. Neither of my parents read my first novel until it was in bound galleys. Jill talked about her mother's support, too. Her mother had kept dozens of scrapbooks with all her father's press clippings, programs, and photographs. Her mother's unconditional focus on her father had made his work possible, she said. In the audience, my mother started to cough.

She was never that kind of wife. She never allowed herself to become my father's number one camp follower. She had seen, although perhaps she didn't know that she had seen, what happens when women let go of their independence even for a moment and allow themselves to be caught up in the excitement of other people's lives. She had seen how quickly an inch can become a mile. In her own family, she had watched as women had lost their professions, their freedom, their health. She knew that the price of combat was too high, and the price of surrender even higher. In the war between men and women, she tried to be a conscientious objector.

Within her family, my mother was always the pretty, impractical, and artistic sister. She was the one everyone could push around, and the one who needed, and got, protection from the harsh outside world. She has a helpless, feminine, do-it-to-me quality, which goes with her high baby-girl voice, a sexy, stunned out-of-it-ness that seems to provoke men—but that also attracts people who live by taking advantage of other people. Not only is she a mark for sick or stray animals, but the back bedroom in my parents' house in Ossining was occasionally occupied by a stray human—a student who didn't want to go home for vacation, a friend who had fought with her husband. "But she has nowhere else to go," my mother would say.

A smile, a few corny presents, the demonstration of need, and a little courtliness are all it takes to activate my mother's easy advocacy of strangers. "He seemed like such a nice man!" she'll say, talking about the gardener who put five thousand extra miles on her car while she was away for a week, or the cleaning lady's boyfriend who made off with her jewelry, or an academic biographer out to enhance his reputation with an "insider's" look at John Cheever's life.

In 1987, one of these "nice" men persuaded her to sign a contract with a little-known Chicago publishing house for what she understood was a limited edition printing of a few of my father's short stories. When she found that the publisher was proceeding to publish a major book including *all* of the stories that had not appeared in the 1978 collection *The Stories of John Cheever*, she couldn't believe it at first. Both the publisher and his representative had seemed so gentlemanly and friendly, if a bit incompetent. It was a profound shock, sustained at the age of seventy, for my mother to find that even "nice" men can be not so nice.

A bruised, spacey absentness is my mother's armor, her fortification, her unbridgeable moat. She is always too busy to talk about her own behavior, or about anything else that might threaten her flaky composure. She's rushing off to the supermarket, or anxious to pick up the mail.

Socially, she's disconcertingly unpredictable. Usually, she's polite and gracious, but she's prone to attacks of candor which can scatter even the most convivial group. "Who is that man with the *huge* nose?" she once exclaimed in her carrying, Bo-Peep voice as Manhattan District Attorney Robert Morgenthau chatted near us at a literary dinner. When, at a party at Ann and Bernard Malamud's apartment in New York, the writer Harold Brodkey told my brother Ben how much my father had loved his children, my mother interrupted. "Oh no," she said in a surprised voice as Ben stood there helplessly. "The only one of the children he ever *really* cared about was Fred!" When a drunken female guest at an Ossining luncheon fell off her terrace and down onto a rocky flower bed, my mother looked down at the apparently unconscious body and gasped. "There go my dahlias!" she said.

As I unravel the tangled oral history which was all I knew about my mother's family and read the boxes of letters my grandfather left in the archives at Yale, my own connection to my mother has come into focus.

"What did I do wrong?" I ask my brother Ben.

"You were born, you were a child, you made impossible

demands on her the way children do," he says. "The trouble with our parents was that they wanted to be the children."

The diminishment and waste my mother saw with her grandmother, her mother, and her sister Buff have also been visited on her. Her children depend on her and complain about her. She lived for us. My father acted as if he owned her, tearing off the intimate fabric of her life and cutting it into shapes and forms to clothe the creatures of his own imagination.

"I certainly let myself be victimized," she tells me now. "But I wanted my family and my home. I wanted those things very much." She pauses for a moment. "I wanted those things very much," she says again.

"Why didn't you kick him out?" I ask.

"Oh Susie, I couldn't," she says. "I just couldn't. I thought of leaving but then I didn't want to end up living in a furnished room somewhere. . . ." Memory drags her backward. "Everyone kept saying that it must be so wonderful to be married to him."

" 'How lucky you are to have him for a father,' " I say. "I know what you mean."

"It was my nature," my mother says, her voice sounding sad to me now. "Being victimized was also in my nature. Do you remember that psychiatrist we sent you to?"

"Dr. Sobel?" I was eleven when I was first taken to a psychiatrist. He had an office in White Plains.

"I remember when your father and I went to see him, he said to your father in this stern voice, 'You married this woman because you knew that you could dominate her!' Your father and I both stood there horrified, drawn together against this man who could say such a dreadful thing."

"He was pretty brassy." The main thing I remember about Dr. Sobel was how shocked I was when he asked if I was menstruating. I wasn't sure what menstruation was.

"He liked you," my mother says. "He said you had a Ford body but a Cadillac engine."

"Frankly," I say, "I would have preferred it the other way around." We both laugh.

When I first married in 1967, my mother and I became friends. It was a time of growth and independence for both of us, and for a while we were both teachers. When I visited my parents at their house in Ossining, my mother and I sat in her bedroom, gossiping and trying on each other's clothes the way mothers and daughters are supposed to. We actually confided in each other, although I never told her the two secrets that shadow those years when I remember them: the fact that I was in love with a married man I worked with, and the fact that my husband occasionally hauled off and hit me so hard that I saw stars and once had a black eye for a week. I told my students and my parents that I had walked into a cupboard door in the kitchen.

My father often said how much my friendship with my mother meant to him. My role was to defend her. This gave him the freedom to attack her. "When M. returns there is the general hurly-burly about supper," he wrote in a typical journal entry about her, "she has too much to do and yet there is no one to help her. I offer to clean the table but I am told that it would be no use; it would only have to be done again. . . . And I think of those marriages that exist as much less than a mere arrangement; a well of despair." The wife in my father's writing complained about her husband while spending his money. She refused his help and complained that no one helped her. She rejected his sexual advances—advances that, he often reminded her, others often welcomed. My advocacy of my mother's position alleviated my father's guilt. My friendship with her also gave me a reason not to want to hear about or meet his other women. It served us all well.

My mother didn't have a mother for long. She holds her infant grandchildren gingerly, as if they might break. As toddlers they make her nervous with their demands and their noise and their sloppiness. Her tolerance for messiness and loudness is low. She treats children the way she was treated as a child; she expects them to be little adults, responsible for their behavior and able to deal with criticism and even sarcasm. It was in seeing her timid handling of my daughter that I began to understand what a stifling burden I must have been for my mother. She was a child herself, and in her family childbearing went along with the black magic of suffering and death.

There was always a lot of confusion in our family about who were the parents and who were the children. My mother often flirted with my boyfriends, and my father made clumsy, embarrassing passes at my brothers' girlfriends. My competition with my mother for my father's attention was also heartbreakingly direct. I often substituted for my mother as a date when my father went to parties. One friend of my father's thrilled me by writing a note saying how much he had enjoyed meeting me even though we—my father and I—weren't married. There was never any distance between us. My parents' way of urging us on was not to cheer for us from the sidelines, but to pull ahead of us.

We children all wished in vain, as my parents had wished in

vain when *they* were children, for the kind of ideal parents we saw on television and read about in comic books—parents who were unstintingly supportive and protective, parents who took care of you. There were moments when my father at least *acted* like the father played by Russell Crouse on the show he sometimes wrote for called *Life with Father.* My mother never even pretended. Still, in their own imperfect way, they did as well as anyone can do at being a parent. They did their best.

Both of them knew the importance of family and both were dedicated to making it work. They taught us, by example, that anxiety and adversity are difficult but bearable, that it's important to follow your gifts and that if you do you will be rewarded although not perhaps in the way you dream. We learned from watching my father that to survive as a writer you have to just keep writing, even when editors turn down your stories, even when there's no money, even when reviewers savage you. My father had a lot of trouble believing in his own ability. His journals are full of self-doubt and sharp criticism of his own work. It was often my mother's unspoken support, her willingness to build a life and a family on the sometimes frail evidence of his talent that kept him going. It is not so extraordinary that my mother is now loyal to my father's work and the way he wanted his work to be perceived. What's extraordinary is that she felt that way even when no one else did, and even when it often meant she and her children had to go without. My father taught me how to be a writer. My mother taught me something even more useful—how to live with a writer.

"It wasn't so much that Mummy and I were competing," I say to my brother Ben when we talk on the telephone. Ben and I call our parents Mummy and Daddy. Fred refers to them as

Mom and Dad. "I think the problem is simpler. I love her and she doesn't love me," I say. "End of story."

"But you're still hoping!" my brother Ben says. I can hear his dogs barking in the background. Someone's ringing his doorbell. My unsuccessful quest for my mother's love is the force that locks us together in our endless dance of sympathy and opposition, the dance of mothers and daughters.

FOURTEEN

ILLNESS FOLLOWED MY MOTHER like a shadow all her life, but she was never sick. My father and I and both my brothers were sick all the time. My father had heart problems and lung problems and all the aches and pains of an alcoholic and a chain-smoker. My brother Ben started life with a major operation on his eye— I remember him as an infant swathed in scary head bandages, and he remained frail. My younger brother Fred had colds and stomachaches. I had terrible asthma, asthma that was brought on by exposure to an animal or cold air or leaf mold or cigarette smoke, but that also flared up for no apparent reason. I could usually feel an attack coming on. There would be a catch and a slow narrowing in my throat, and I could sense the bronchial tubes closing. My shoulders went back and I leaned forward in order to breathe. A harsh wheezing sound came from my chest as I fought for air. Each attack seemed endless, and as I felt more desperate, I breathed harder. Sometimes the doctor rushed over and gave me a shot of cortisone. Sometimes I took pills and that helped. I slept propped up against the pillows, bending forward to suck air into the diminishing space in my lungs.

My mother is an inspired nurse. She never lost her temper with my asthma attacks or suggested that I was avoiding school or that my illness was psychological—even when I had an attack on Sunday night, as I often did. When I was sick she brought me presents, books, and magazines, and cooked whatever I said I might be able to eat—usually bland foods like noodles and potatoes—things she would snap at me for even thinking about eating when I wasn't sick.

It wasn't just a bedside manner. It was also that my parents—speaking through my mother—made their most important concessions when I was sick. I was hunched over in bed to ease my wheezing when they extended my bedtime from eight to midnight and when they said I could go away to boarding school. I was in bed when my mother said they would "think about" buying me my first car.

"They took illness seriously," my mother tells me when we're talking about her parents. No wonder! Both of Helen's brothers had died of childhood diseases; Helen and Winter were both doctors. My mother's memories of being sick are eerily like my own. She recalls the delicious sounds of a parent moving solicitously around the room as she drifted off into sleep. "When I had the flu," she says, "both my parents were worrying about me and sponging me off and taking care of me. It was wonderful. It's amazing that I didn't become a hypochondriac." Instead, she married one.

"Bill is a wonderful nurse," my Uncle Bill's wife says. "He's wonderful when anyone is sick." It's late at night in their living room in the Alabama woods. Bill is telling me that his mother never inflicted her pain on her children, even when she was dying. Two dogs stretch out on the floor. Bill picks a grape off a bunch in a pottery bowl and feeds it to the black and white dog, the dog named Grace. His wife dozes in the shadows of the room near the window looking out over the dark lake.

My father's mother had been a practicing Christian Scientist. She believed in prayer rather than in medicine. She did not call a doctor when my father was sick. She did not call one when she broke her own leg. My father was always on the brink of illness. He had a racking smoker's cough. He had bursitis and stiff muscles and intestinal problems. Beginning in his forties he often joked that he was "an old man, nearing the end of his journey." This was a threatening joke for us. Once every few years he landed in the hospital for a minor operation or as the result of an accident.

Then in 1972, almost ten years after my mother began fighting to establish herself in a life outside their marriage, he got so sick that it changed everything for her. There was a small heart attack and, in the spring of 1973, a major heart attack. Confined to a hospital bed in cardiac care, unable to get any liquor, my father suffered through a two-day bout of delirium tremens which, combined with the heart attack, almost killed him. For a few months he stopped drinking, but by the winter of 1973 he was teaching at Boston University and drinking again. At the age of sixty-one, he went completely out of control. He took long walks in the Boston winter without an overcoat. He almost froze to death, he said. He failed to show up for classes, or showed up and spoke incoherently. He announced that he had tried to commit suicide. He was picked up by the police for drunken loitering. In the spring of 1974, he finally entered a rehabilitation center.

My father's illness hit at a time when his family was scattering. My brother Ben and I had both married. Fred was away at school. My mother was teaching and writing poetry. My father's collapse and the decade after it, during which his health was always in jeopardy, brought the family back together and re-created our intense focus on him.

After he came out of the rehabilitation center, my father stopped drinking, but we were always painfully aware of the fragility of his sobriety—and the deadly consequences if he were to drink again. Then, in early 1980, he had an unexplained seizure. He was put on Dilantin, an antiseizure drug, which caused depression. Then there was another seizure. The next spring he entered the local hospital to have a kidney removed.

One result of my father's sickness was that he recaptured my mother's attention. Sometimes it seemed like an exhausted truce, as if in forty years they had just worn each other out, but at other times they really seemed to be friends.

"Your father is a very special person," my mother told me as we stood in a hospital corridor outside one of the rooms where he stayed in those years. I was amazed; I had never heard her say anything like that before. My mother's anger seemed to evaporate in the face of my father's pain and helplessness.

The operation to remove my father's kidney accelerated his final illness. During surgery the urologist cut through a tumor that later tests showed was malignant. The doctor kept this to himself. Doctors don't like to give bad news. When I found out later that the doctor had failed to report the malignancy when it might have been early enough to treat it successfully, I urged my mother to sue. Her brother Bill, who had been monitoring my father's case, also urged her to bring a complaint against the doctor. My mother would sigh whenever I brought this up. "Oh Susie," she would say. "That's all water under the bridge."

"But what if he does it to someone else!" I would argue. "Just for that reason you should at least file a complaint against him." My mother would sigh again and change the subject. She had something on the stove. The dogs had to be let out or in. A neighbor had dropped by and she couldn't talk.

Later that summer, in August of 1981, when my mother had gone up to Treetops and I was about to leave for a two-week trip to France, I went out to visit my father in Ossining. We drove across the street to swim at his friend Sara Spencer's pool. As we walked across Sara's velvety lawn toward the pool, she held me back for a moment.

"Don't leave him alone," she said. "Don't go."

"I'm not leaving him alone," I said. "He has you." What I meant was that I was thirty-eight years old and that my father would have to take care of himself somehow. Of course he couldn't take care of himself.

In the fall, my father was suddenly much sicker. He went to the family doctor, who told him that the cancer which had originated in his kidneys had now spread to his bones and that he had less than a year to live.

My mother and my brother Ben and his wife had tickets for *Nicholas Nickleby* on Broadway that night. I was in California. As people often do when struck by disaster, they continued with their plans as if nothing had happened. After the theater, my brother and his wife went home and my mother spent the night alone in my New York apartment as we had planned. Later she told my brother that it was the worst night of her life. She told me that she had trouble finding the bathtub plug and couldn't take a bath.

All through the six months of my father's last illness, my mother was calm and loving. When we found out he was going to die, she moved him back into the master bedroom with her, from the guest room off the hall to which he had been banished years ago. The drugs my father had to take threw him into ugly moods which were like his old drunken moods. He was sarcastic and volatile. He did not want to die. My mother tolerated his complaints and his stoicism. She bolstered his moments of hope and comforted him through moments of despair. She didn't try to push him to accept his condition, but she made it clear that she accepted it. She welcomed and cooked for the stream of visitors who came to say good-bye to him, gently and gracefully allowing them to deny that that was what they had come for. She fed him the runny cereal that was often all he could eat after the chemotherapy he took, and she drove him back and forth from the hospital dozens of times.

When he died, at the end of a hot afternoon in June, she was lying next to him on the bed in the master bedroom. "Don't cry," she told us. "We have our memories of him." In the chaos that followed, as the room filled with policemen and the coroner's men and the minister, and the telephone began to ring, I noticed that my mother was sitting quietly in a corner talking intently to my brother Ben, who was holding both her hands. I couldn't hear what she was saying.

"That won't happen, Mummy," I could hear him saying as he leaned toward her. Later he told me that she was asking him to make sure that she didn't die the way my father had died. My mother has been well acquainted with death for a long time. She didn't want us to go through what she had just been through, she was saying. She didn't want to have to be nursed herself.

FIFTEEN

DURING THE 1950s my parents went out for dinner once or twice a week, leaving me and my toddler brother Ben with a gray-haired battle-ax named Mrs. Smith. A square woman who spoke in pieties like "money isn't everything" and "you get more flies with honey than vinegar," Mrs. Smith adored my brother, and she and I tried to avoid open conflict.

Upstairs in my parents' bedroom after they were safely out of the driveway, I would shut the door and sprawl in my mother's upholstered chair, sucking a candy from her dish of peppermints on the table and leafing through whatever book she happened to be reading. The rich smell of that room, part flowery perfume and powder, part cigarettes and whiskey, allayed my keen sense of my parents' absence. I would stand in front of my mother's flower-skirted dressing table and stare at myself in her triptych of mirrors, pulling my hair back with her silver brushes and tortoiseshell combs and imagining myself as a grown woman. I would systematically go through the closets and the desk drawers, looking for chocolate, for hidden presents if it was close to my birthday or a major holiday, and for information. I lived at home like a guerrilla in an occupied town, always alert to anything that might affect my life.

One night when my father had just published *The Enormous Radio*, his second collection of short stories, I noticed a copy with its gleaming new black and yellow dustcover lying on my parents' bed. Idly, knowing somehow that I was breaking the rules but not really knowing why, I began to flip through the pages. There were the stories I had heard people talking about at parties where I was allowed to pass the peanuts and ask if my father could sweeten anyone's drink, and the stories I had noticed in passing while looking at the cartoons in *The New Yorker*. The book fell open to a story called "The Hartleys." My interest increased as I began reading what was clearly, to me, an account of a ski trip our family had taken to Vermont with two other families, the Kahns and the Reimans, the previous year.

On the trip we had all driven up to South Woodstock, Vermont, in three cars and stayed at Hyacinth House, a yellow brick bed and breakfast across from the post office. I enjoyed skiing, but by our third day in Vermont, I developed a bad case of asthma. For the rest of our stay, I lay in bed, drifting in and out of a benedryl-induced sleep. I only heard about an accident that Ginger Reiman, one of my parents' friends, had on our last day of skiing. Her ski sweater got caught in the old rope tow at Mount Tom, and she was dragged a few yards up the snowy hill before she could free herself.

In the short story I was reading, a couple, the Hartleys, go on a ski trip alone with their seven-year-old daughter. My heart beat faster as I read, thrilled and a little scared by the eerie parallels between myself and this little girl in a book.

At the end of the short story, Anne Hartley, the little girl in the book, gets her arm caught in the rope tow and is brutally dragged to her death. "Her screams were hoarse and terrible," I read, "and the more she struggled to free herself from the rope, the more violently it threw her to the ground. . . . The girl's cries were piercing until her neck was broken on the iron wheel."

The world stopped when I read the end of that story, and when it started again it wasn't quite the same. Looking up I saw a shabby room in a small, dark house, furnished with a sagging bed and a tawdry dressing table. Quickly I plumped up the cushions on my mother's chair to erase my presence at the scene and placed the book back on the bed exactly where I had found it. Then I left the room, shutting the door carefully behind me, and went downstairs to argue with Mrs. Smith about my bedtime.

Years later, I got up the nerve to ask my father why he had written a story like that. He said that he had been expressing his anxieties about me. He told me that Ginger Reiman's accident had triggered his fears about my getting hurt while skiing. I didn't believe him. I don't think he was expressing anxieties about me; I don't think he was expressing a secret wish to see me dead, either. "The Hartleys" is fiction, a story, and I don't think my father thought about anything while he was writing it except what would make a good story, if he thought about anything at all.

I certainly wasn't the only member of our family or of our community to have their personal details pop up in my father's stories. Of course, the characters and events in the stories are not real, they are invented—yet scenes and details in my father's work were often completely familiar to anyone who lived with him, or sometimes to anyone who knew him.

"Oh, your wicked husband," Frank Vanderlip said to my mother when they met years after my father died. The Vanderlips were convinced that my father had moved to the little house on their estate in order to write about their family, their mansion, and their scandals. *The Wapshot Chronicle* did little to shake their conviction. Again and again the details of our lives and our neighbors' lives turned up in the public pages of *The New Yorker*, sandwiched between the Peter Arno cartoons and the ads for New England inns.

It was my mother whose physical characteristics and emotional complexities appeared in the female characters in almost everything my father wrote after they met in 1939 until the last story he wrote in 1981. For more than forty years my mother was my father's principal resource for the description of women. Sometimes it's hard for us to separate who she really is from the dozens of literary portraits my father created. She was his everywoman, his raw material for the female characters in his stories and novels, and his one-woman university for the study of female motives and female behavior.

My father liked his women pretty and he liked them gentle. When women in his fiction step outside their rigidly defined sexual roles—roles as adoring and beautiful wives or nurturing mothers—they are punished. My father argued that this fear of unfeminine women came from his bad experiences with his mother. It was certainly lived out in his marriage. My mother put up with this odd situation for most of her life. She tried never to fight with my father because, she said, her angry words always ended up in a short story. What made his use of domestic and intimate personal details even harder was that most readers didn't even bother to make the distinction between fact and fiction.

"Oh, Mary," a neighbor once said when my mother ran into her at the supermarket after the publication of "O Youth and Beauty," a story about an aging athlete who tried to regain his youth by running drunken steeplechases over the furniture, "I didn't know that John had been a track star." In fact the athlete in the story, Cash Bentley, reminded us all of another neighbor, Dudley Schoales, and the way, late at night, he would show off his fading athletic prowess by vaulting over the furniture without spilling his whiskey. Not only did readers assume that fiction was fact, they usually even got that wrong.

※

Writing played a central role in the seesaw of anger and affection that characterized my parents' marriage. My mother had started out at Sarah Lawrence as a promising young poet, and in the 1960s she began to write poetry again—poetry that sometimes included a monstrous, oblivious husband or an adored, absent lover. At the same time, she was teaching creative writing. She would occasionally bring home a piece written by one of her students. "Now this is a wonderful story," she would proclaim, urging us all to read pages of wooden collegiate prose. "This is how a story *should* be constructed." My father didn't take this very well. But by the 1970s, when their marriage had somehow expanded to accommodate both his sobriety and his bisexuality, they had made a kind of peace.

During this time, more than a decade after her first teaching

job, my mother took a position with *Westchester*, a local magazine run by the wives of a group of businessmen. She quickly
realized that she had been hired because the editors hoped she
would bring in "important" fiction in general and stories by
John Cheever in particular. Obligingly, my father wrote a story
for the magazine titled "The Night Mummy Got the Wrong
Mink Coat." My father had just bought my mother her first
mink coat. In the story the narrator's wife leaves a dance at the
country club only to find when she slips her hands into its
pockets that she is wearing someone else's mink coat. The story
is a benevolent scrutiny of suburban society and of what pos-
sessions and the language of possession can mean. My father
signed it with a pseudonym—Louisa Spingarn.

My mother turned the story in without comment. The editors, assuming Louisa Spingarn to be a dowdy suburban friend
of my mother's, were reluctant to publish it. Who was this
Louisa Spingarn anyway? they asked.

She's a sort of latter-day Emily Dickinson," my mother told
them. It was too much of a "woman's piece" for the magazine,
they said. There were some nice touches, one editor admitted,
but the story was short for *Westchester*. Could Louisa Spingarn
expand it? My mother said that Louisa Spingarn would not
rewrite. The story was rejected. All this caused tremendous
hilarity back at the homestead. No one knows how the editors
of *Westchester* felt when and if they came upon "The Night
Mummy Got the Wrong Mink Coat" in the pages of *The New
Yorker* later that year. My mother had left the job before that
happened.

For readers who disregarded my father's frequent announcement that "fiction is not crypto-autobiography" and insisted on reducing his work to relate to the facts of his life, my mother was often eminently recognizable in his work. My father sometimes seemed to be using his stories to communicate with her. Their fights over her allegiance to her family, her summer trips to Treetops, her understandable sexual reluctance, her absentmindedness in the kitchen, and most of all her efforts through work and friendship to establish a life of her own, all were transformed into the stuff of fiction.

In *Falconer*, the hero Ezekial Farragut's first visitor after he goes to prison for the murder of his brother is his beautiful wife Marcia. When Farragut asks if his son Peter can visit him, Marcia answers vaguely, then changes the subject.

"Oh, dammit," she said. Peevishness darkened her face. "Oh, Goddammit," she said with pure indignation.

"What's wrong?" he asked.

"I can't find my Kleenex," she said. She was foraging in the bag.

"I'm sorry," he said.

"Everything seems to fight me today," she said, "absolutely everything." She dumped the contents of her bag onto the counter.

"Lady, lady," said the turnkey, who sat above them on an elevated chair like a lifeguard. "Lady, you ain't allowed to have nothing on the counter but soft drinks and butt cans."

"I," she said, "am a taxpayer. I help to support this place. It costs me more to keep my husband in here than it costs me to send my son to a good school."

"Lady, lady, please," he said. "Get that stuff off the counter or I'll have to kick you out."

She found the small box of paper. . . . Then he covered her hand with his, deeply thrilled at this recollection of his past. She pulled her hand away, but why? Had she let him touch her for a minute, the warmth, the respite, would have lasted for weeks.

Farragut is confined in a seven-by-twelve-foot cell. Chagrined but willing, he listens to Marcia talk about her trip to Jamaica and humors her claims that she might have had and might still have a career as a painter. He tolerates her manipulation of their joint checking account and her insistence that he has ruined her life by marrying her.

" 'And how,' Farragut asks Marcia on the other side of the bars, 'is the house? How is Indian Hill?' He did not use the possessive pronoun—My house, Your house, Our house. . . . She didn't reply. She did not draw on her gloves finger by finger, or touch her hair, or resort to any of the soap opera chestnuts used to express contempt. She was sharper than that. 'Well,' she said, 'it's nice to have a dry toilet seat.' " It is Marcia's coldness toward Farragut that leads to his passionate prison affair with another male inmate.

Sometimes the women in my father's work are feminine and yielding, but more often they are self-indulgent and vain, willing to emasculate their men and abandon their children.

❧

In "An Educated American Woman," it is Jill Madison's insistence on her independence and her interest in the local highway commission that cause the neglect of her husband and the abuse through negligence of her son Bibber. She's at a highway commission meeting one evening when her husband Georgie comes home to find their son alone, in bed, fatally ill. "He wrapped the boy in a blanket and carried him down the stairs, enormously grateful to have this much to do. The ambulance was there in a few minutes.

"Jill had stopped long enough to have a drink with one of her assistants and came in half an hour later. 'Hail the conquering hero!' she called as she stepped into the empty house. 'We shall have our hearing and the scurvy rascals are on the run.' " Her little son, of course, is dead.

After my mother's job at Briarcliff Junior College ended, she took other teaching jobs. One of these, at the Rockland Country Day School across the Hudson, led to an appearance in an amateur theatrical performance. In the performance my mother played a character who takes part in a mock wedding. My father attended the performance—under duress. When, during the service on stage, the actor/preacher asked if anyone knew of any impediment to the marriage, my father stood up in the audience and created a major disturbance. Yes, he thundered, glaring at the local players in this two-bit theatrical, the wedding should not take place because the bride was already married—to him! My father was quite a famous man, and his performance more than eclipsed the performances of my mother and her amateur colleagues.

A few months later he wrote "The Fourth Alarm," a story in which the narrator's wife Bertha, "a good-looking young woman with a splendid figure," takes a teaching job after her children are old enough to go to school. The teaching job leads to membership in an amateur theatrical group, and the amateur theatrical group leads to an audition for a nude show called *Ozamanides II*. Bertha tells her husband she will be nude on stage and simulate having sex with other actors and members of the audience. She is thrilled with her new career. " 'Oh, I'm so happy,' the mother of his children tells him. 'Oh how wonderful and rich and strange life can be when you stop playing out the roles that your parents and their friends wrote out for you. I feel like an explorer.' "

Bertha's husband attends her performance—under duress. After a few scenes he leaves the theater and walks out onto Broadway in the falling snow. He remembers that he has snow tires. "This gave me a sense of security and accomplishment that would have disgusted Ozamanides and his naked court. . . . The wind flung the snow into my face and so, singing and jingling the car keys, I walked to the train."

In story after story, my mother's quest for a life outside her marriage is exaggerated into a grotesque and baffling absurdity.

"I had important ambitions," screams Zena in "The Chimera." "I might have been a businesswoman, a TV writer, a politician, an actress. I might have been a congresswoman!"

"I didn't know you wanted to be a congresswoman," her sweet-natured husband replies.

"That's the trouble with you. You never think of me. You never think of what I might have done. You've ruined my life!"

Another wife, Cora Fry in "The Ocean," has a voice "in the octave above middle C" and a disconcerting absentmindedness in the kitchen. When her husband spits out his salad at dinner because of its odd taste, she allows that she must have mistaken his lighter fluid for vinegar. He is afraid she's trying to poison him. In another scene, he walks into the kitchen while she's cooking.

> Cora was at the table, bending over a dish of cutlets. In one hand she held a can of lethal pesticide. . . . She was startled when I came in, and by the time I had my glasses on she had put the pesticide on the table. . . . It contained a high percentage of nerve poison. "What in the world are you doing?" I asked.
>
> "What does it look as if I were doing?" she asked, still speaking in the octave above middle C.
>
> "It looks as if you were putting pesticide in the cutlets," I said.
>
> "I know you don't grant me much intelligence," she said, "but please grant me enough intelligence to know better than that."
>
> "But what are you doing with the pesticide?" I asked.
>
> "I have been dusting the roses," she said.

In "The Geometry of Love," Mathilda Mallory is a self-centered woman who visits her dying husband in the hospital, spills the soup on him, and worries about the spot it makes on her skirt. In "Torch Song," Joan Harris is a woman whose relationships with men inevitably lead to sickness and death— their sickness and death. At the end of the story the narrator, Jack Lorey, knows that he's in trouble when Joan comes to visit him.

> " 'Get out,' he said.
>
> " 'You're sick, darling,' she said. 'I can't leave you alone here.'

" 'Get out,' he said again. . . . 'What kind of an obscenity are you that you can smell sickness and death the way you do?'

" 'You poor darling.'

" 'Does it make you feel young to watch the dying?' he shouted. 'Is that the lewdness that keeps you young?' "

Joan leaves, saying she'll be back at nightfall. In terror, Lorey packs and escapes. "He emptied the ashtray containing his nail parings and cigarette butts into the toilet, and swept the floor with a shirt, so that there would be no trace of his life, of his body, when that lewd and searching shape of death came there to find him in the evening."

"They had burned veal on Sunday, burned meat loaf on Monday, and on Tuesday the meat was so burned that Seton couldn't guess what it was," my father wrote in a story called "The Music Teacher." At an earlier meal in the story, the meat was also burned. "So was almost everything else—the rolls, the potatoes, and the frozen apple tart. There were cinders in Seton's mouth and a great heaviness in his heart as he looked past the plates of spoiled food to Jessica's face, once gifted with wit and passion but now dark and lost to him." To Seton, it seems that the burned food and the wails of his three children that greet him when he arrives are planned, arranged by his wife to disconcert him at the moment of his homecoming.

"I didn't think about it, or I didn't read them," my mother tells me when I ask her how she felt about my father's use of her in the stories. "It didn't bother me much except for the story about the woman who burned all the food, remember that one? I was afraid everyone would think that I burned the food, and I didn't . . . at least not often."

Burning food was the least of it. A story that went too far
even for my mother was "An Educated American Woman." As
my brothers, my mother, and quite a few other people perceived, the energy for the story came from anger, a fierce anger
at what my father perceived as my mother's abandonment of
her proper role as wife and mother.

"He didn't have to kill that little boy," my mother says, her
voice rising although the story was first published twenty-five
years ago. "He didn't!" Later, she tells me about a day she left
Fred, her little boy, my younger brother, at home with a cold
because she had to go to work. She left him alone . . . with my
father. My father wrote in a room downstairs and Fred's bedroom was at the top of the house. There was no question of my
father staying upstairs with Fred. My mother gave Fred a pot
lid and a wooden spoon and told him to bang the spoon against
the lid if he needed to signal his father.

"Did you fight about it?" I ask, when we're talking about "An
Educated American Woman."

"There was no point in talking to your father about it," my
mother says. "But I did ask Bill Maxwell why he had to kill that
little boy." Bill Maxwell was my father's editor at *The New Yorker.*

"What did he say?"

"He said, oh well, he just did. It was necessary."

My mother wasn't the only person upset by the story. "No
one likes Bibber's demise," my father wrote, in June 1965, to his
Russian friend and confidante Tanya Litvinov in response to
her protests, "but that's the way it was written and I think that's
the way it should stay." Then he explained away my mother's
complaints in a way that was both completely right and completely wrong.

"It comes down, I guess, to an autobiographical grudge," he wrote. "When I was eleven I was attacked by a virulent strain of tuberculosis. A few days after the crisis my mother covered me in a blanket, gave me a pile of clean rags on which I might bleed, and . . . went off to chairman some committee for the General Welfare. As a healthy man I expect I should be grateful to be alive and to have had so conscientious a parent, but what I would like to forget is the empty house and the fear of death.

"The President of the United States has asked me to dine with him on Tuesday. . . ."

When he was in his forties, my father had discovered that he may have had childhood tuberculosis from an X ray taken as part of a checkup. Tanya, of course, didn't know that. Certainly the anguish of abandonment my father felt whenever my mother tried to do something on her own was a resonance from earlier painful separations from his own mother. His suffering was unreasonable, but it was intense, and real enough to power his evocations of empty houses and innocent deaths.

My father remembered everything that happened to him. Things that caused him pain he remembered with excruciating vividness. It all went into his memory and came back out shaped by his tremendous talent into moving fictional incidents, scenes, and conversations. I think he remembered without even knowing that he remembered. He absorbed everything, from the Vanderlip family secrets to my desperate homesickness at camp, which became Bibber's homesickness at camp in "An Educated American Woman," to my mother's use of food and cooking as a means of expression; and he used everything. But instead of beating swords into plowshares, as he often urged us to do during family fights, he beat plowshares into swords. These verbal weapons were then collected from *The New Yorker* and other magazines into volumes of short stories, and many of them, including "The Hartleys" and "An Educated American Woman," were finally bound together in the best-selling, critically acclaimed, Pulitzer Prize–winning *Stories of John Cheever.* When my mother tells me about her chance meeting with Frank Vanderlip, we laugh about the Vanderlips' certainty that he was writing about them. My mother is silent for a moment. "Maybe he *was* wicked," she says.

SIXTEEN

My FATHER REFUSED to discuss the relationship between his life and the life of characters in his fiction. Suggestions that his or other writers' characters were modeled on real people infuriated him. "You are reducing literature to gossip," he would say. My mother never publicly contradicted him. In fact the connection between life and art, reality and invention, is profound and complicated beyond explanation. "I object greatly to this taking people's lives and putting them into fiction," says a character to the writer in Philip Roth's novel *Deception* in a dialogue that might have taken place between my mother, if she had been bolder, and my father, if he had been more honest. "And then being a famous author who resents critics for saying that he doesn't make things up."

"Because you had a baby doesn't mean I didn't make up a baby," the writer tells his character, "because you're you doesn't mean I didn't make *you* up."

"I also exist."

"Also. You also exist and I also made you up. 'Also' is a good word to remember. You also don't exist as only you."

"I certainly don't anymore."

My mother understood the unfathomable nature of the writing process, and she is as angry as he would have been when critics try to read his work as if it were crypto-autobiography. Whatever price she paid for nurturing it, my mother believed in my father's genius. My brothers, who were also involuntary sources for him, are not so restrained.

❧

"There's absolutely no excuse for what he did with Mom," my brother Fred says. "He did it on purpose. Vindictiveness was one of the characteristics that he displayed in his art." Fred is the child my father loved the best. My father wanted him to go to law school; Fred wanted to get a doctorate in Spanish history. When my father died, Fred went to law school—and, to his surprise, he loved it. Now he's a lawyer in Denver.

"What he did is a major wrong. It's right up there with slavery," Fred tells me on the telephone. "I don't know why she didn't leave. She's one of the toughest people I know, but I have the awful feeling that the reason she stayed was us kids."

"But if the stories are great," I say, "doesn't that make a difference?"

"Art is no license," Fred says, talking fast as if he hadn't heard me. "There is no freedom from human obligations. Otherwise you're saying that some lives are more valuable than others. You end up with a society in which real live people are sacrificed for art."

"It wasn't just what he wrote," my brother Ben says, when I

ask him about this. "He *told* terrible stories about us, too. People are always coming up to me and saying, 'So you're the little boy who got his penis caught in his zipper!' "

"At least that was funny."

"Not to me!" Ben says. "It wasn't funny then and it's not very funny now. It was his credo that any sacrifice was worth it for a good story—or even a good crack."

"What's your credo?" I ask. Ben has just finished writing his first novel.

"Language is a pistol," he says. "A pistol is a fine thing if you use it to defend yourself, or for robbing from the rich if you are poor. It's not so fine if you shoot your little son and daughter with it."

"He didn't always get away with it," I say. "He fought with the Vanderlips, and Mummy was upset about 'An Educated American Woman.' "

"But now he's perceived as a saint," Ben says. "And you'd better watch out what you say about a saint."

"Everyone he hurt is beyond protest," I say. "He waited them out. What's literary libel in 1950 is literary genius in 1990."

"I think there is such a thing as going on stage and cutting your son or daughter in half, and then going backstage and hugging them and explaining that you love them—that cutting them is just what you do for a living."

"But he didn't do that."

"He couldn't," Ben says. "Whatever he did was necessary to his survival and he never stopped doing it. The trouble is that I've ended up feeling as if I was a minor character in someone else's book."

"Aaaargh," I say.

"I think it's important somehow that he was homosexual," my brother says. "He was always dealing in secrets. There's a level of deception required for homosexuals that the rest of us just can't understand."

"What does that have to do with fiction?"

"He didn't even think about telling us until he was dying. He kept that secret well."

"He wanted to go to heaven," I say.

Ben sighs, tired of the effort of remembering, and of the effort of forgetting. "You know, I hope he does go to heaven," he says.

"So, do you think he was a monster?" I ask a friend who has just finished writing a novel.

"I'm not going to say what I think, because it would be too strong," she says. "What's worse is that he didn't protect you, and your mother didn't protect you."

"She had her own problems," I say.

"Still you were her children." My friend lies back against the pillows of the sofa and cradles a coffee cup in her hand. Winter sun streams through the windows of her townhouse onto her 1930s retro furniture, a pile of books on psychoanalysis, and the record albums left behind by her late lover the rock singer. "Maybe that's what was wrong with my novel," she says, "maybe I invented too much. Maybe I should have used real people."

My third husband's in the kitchen making the morning coffee when I ask him. "There's nothing wrong with what your father did in those stories," he says. "*You* can't make a decision about that anyway, you have a vested interest." He pours the beans into the top of the grinder. "We couldn't use you as a witness in a court of law," he says.

"You don't think a writer should be bound by any rules at all?" I ask over the noise of the grinder.

"Just what he can get away with," my husband says. He opens the filter and taps the ground coffee into it, leaving a ring of coffee on the counter. "Don't you think you're a little oversensitive?"

"We were children!"

"Children don't read *The New Yorker*."

"You don't think that a ten-year-old girl reading a story by her father in which she's ground to death in a ski tow should be upset?"

"I don't see why that matters," he says.

"You're taking the most extreme position."

"A fiction writer doesn't have that kind of obligation to the few people in his family. He writes for readers."

My husband has never been negatively written about in fiction—never seen his intimate physical and emotional flaws skewered on the page to create a character. I don't think he'd like it. But as we talk, I realize that I have always agreed with the extreme position he's taking. I have never worried too much about the feelings of people who might be able—or inclined—to recognize themselves in my fiction. I steadfastly maintain that I invent my characters. This is true. I do. It's also true that I sometimes invent them out of reality, stitching together scraps and bolt ends of cloth gathered from my experience with people. These scraps and bolt ends are sometimes identifiable. I realize as I argue with my husband that I take what my father did with his family as a license for what I do.

"I think it's all right if the people you use don't mind," another friend says.

"No," I say. "If someone doesn't mind if you murder them, that doesn't make it all right to murder them." I think of my mother.

Even my friends who should know better often assume that fiction I've written can be read as if it were a journal or a diary. One writer admitted to me that she hadn't liked my husband . . . until she read about him in my last novel.

Art is long and life is short, they say. The repercussions of a writer's work on family and friends is very brief compared to the life of a great novel. Who remembers the women who inspired Becky Sharp or Lizzie Eustace or Nicole Diver? Already many of the friends and family whose lives my father used to fashion his stories are dead or moved away or too old to care. He has become a certified literary genius. Some of the stories are great, as good as stories can be. They sing. They dip and soar like swallows at twilight. Everyone has forgotten that there were neighbors who wouldn't talk to him, friends who turned against him, an angry brother, an unhappy wife, and a cleaning lady who threatened to sue.

"What about nonfiction," I ask my husband, who has now settled down with his coffee and the seven newspapers from three cities which are his morning reading.

"The only obligation of nonfiction is accuracy," he says, sipping the coffee from one of the willowware cups I brought down from Treetops at the end of the summer to remind me of sunlit days and the sweetness of the air.

"Accuracy! Accuracy is meaningless," I say. He turns a page of the *Washington Post.* "You can be accurate and destroy someone or you can be accurate and write a puff about them. It just depends on which facts you choose to be accurate with."

"That's an absurd definition of accuracy," he says.

"Would you say that Grandpa Watson's story about Bell spilling the acid on his hand when they invented the telephone was accurate?" I ask.

"Of course," my husband says.

SEVENTEEN

THE LAST TIME my father went to Treetops was for my twenty-eighth birthday party in 1971. My birthday, on July 31, had always been a major Treetops production. I was Winter's first grandchild. I remember my discomfort as summer after summer I was scrubbed clean and stuffed into an elaborate party dress, and my terror at the ring of grown-up faces peering down at me as they sang a tipsy version of "Happy birthday, dear Susie," in ragged unison.

By 1971 I was a married woman with a paying job as a newspaper reporter and I had celebrated my birthday in a lot of other places. It was a small party. My father knew I was a fan of *New Yorker* cartoonist Ed Koren, and he surprised me with a drawing Koren had done at his request featuring a crowd of furry creatures shouting "Happy Birthday, Susie." Michael Casey, whose family had bought Pete Charron's farmhouse at the top of the hill, came down to Apple and read his poems about Vietnam, which had just won the Yale Series of Younger

Poets Award. My parents stayed in Hemlock. In honor of this rare visit by my father, my mother installed a pleated plastic door between Hemlock's narrow bedroom with sagging twin beds and its tiny dark bathroom. He was polite. My husband and I drove him home to Ossining the next day. Our car was small, and he ended up in the backseat with the dogs and a bottle of whiskey.

My father was fifty-nine years old that year, but because of drinking and chain-smoking he already had the ailments, discomforts, and selective memory of an old man. He remembered Treetops as a glorious place where pretty women in summer dresses flirted with distinguished men over martinis, a place where the family had lived like royalty and he had been a prince. Sleeping in a sagging bed in a chilly, narrow room and sitting in the back of a small car were not easy for him. He would never go back to Treetops, he said. He never did.

❧

Winter had left the Stone House to Polly for her lifetime, but in 1975, three years before she died, she deeded it over to the Winternitz children—my mother and her two brothers, Tom and Bill, and her surviving sister, Jane. My mother says the Whitneys stripped the house before they left it, taking furniture and china that had always been there and that belonged there. The Whitneys saw it differently. To them, the Stone House was Polly's house, which she generously turned over. It was fitting for her to take with her some of the things she had lived with there for more than forty years. After Winter died, she had moved back from Washington, D.C., to a small apartment on Prospect Street in New Haven, up the hill from the old house at 210 Prospect Street, which had been sold and turned into dentists' offices after Winter died.

In deeding the Stone House to Polly only for her lifetime, Winter made an important decision about the future of Treetops, and he made it in favor of his own children. To him their claims, and the claims of the Watson line, weighed more heavily than the claims of the Whitneys, who had been using Treetops for their summers for as long as they could remember. If he had simply left the Stone House to Polly, her children would have inherited it, and the Winternitz and Whitney children would have had to share Treetops forever. Instead, he made sure that the Whitneys would only be coming to Treetops to stay at the Winternitz children's invitation—an invitation that, of course, was never extended.

The Winternitz children are incapable of sympathy for Polly. She was married to their father for almost thirty years. She spent four decades of summers at Treetops. Still, in the minds of Winter's children she was always a treacherous, self-serving imposter. The Whitneys remember those Treetops years as just another pleasant interlude in their always pleasant lives, while my mother and her brothers and sister still tell their obsessive stories about the Whitneys' greed and the Whitneys' deceptive charm and the Whitneys' snobbishness. The Whitneys never talk about the Winternitz children; their conversation about Treetops is a lot of jolly stories about jolly times in their jolly youth. Janie Whitney Hotchkiss tells me amusing anecdotes about her mother's rudeness when Winter's family came to visit. Stevie Whitney, now retired from Andover, tells me a story about a tennis match on the Treetops court with his brother Freddy. Freddy appeared for the first serve dressed entirely in Polly's clothes, ornate hat and all, and Stevie was so distracted by this androgynous apparition that his excellent game went completely to pieces.

After Polly deeded the Stone House over to the Winternitz children, the Whitneys were kicked off the place—a place that had been as much a part of their childhood as of ours. They never mention this. As Polly explained to Winter in 1934 when he was removed from the deanship of the medical school he had built, the "right" people don't make a fuss. If they lose, the "right" people maintain their dignity by pretending that the loss doesn't matter. The Whitneys don't relive the inglorious past. If they did, they would remember it as glorious.

🌿

At the end of Polly's last summer in the Stone House, after she had left Treetops for good, I went down and let myself in through the heavy wooden front door with its brass plaque "Dr. Milton C. Winternitz," which my father had had made in Rome as a gift for Winter and Polly. The air was stale and smelled of dust and dried flowers and Polly's lavender sachets. It was haunted by Polly and her past and our past together, the echoes of ice in the martini shaker on a hot afternoon, the click of dice shaking in the leather backgammon cups, the laughing voices of the men and women now dead or gone. The heavy silk curtains were drawn, a layer of fragrant dust had settled on the chairs and sofa, and there were still blank spots against the wall where the corner cupboard and round table had been—the furniture that went to New Haven.

It was the next spring before I got up the nerve to sleep in the Stone House. As I sat in Winter's big armchair in the corner of the living room that night, I heard a rustling against the floor in the study. A large yellow rat walked slowly out into the room, glared at me with a mixture of curiosity and disdain, and then hopped up the stairs one at a time, scurried down the balcony, and disappeared into Winter's bedroom. The next night he appeared again, hopped down the stairs, and stalked into the kitchen. During the afternoon, as I sat reading in the sun on the terrace above the lily pond, a huge gleaming copperhead snake slithered out from the cracks in the terra-cotta tiles and coiled next to Polly's white painted iron lawn chair. At night, lying in Polly's four-poster, I could hear animals fighting and screaming a few feet above my face, on the other side of the thin plaster-board ceiling that separated the bedroom from the terra incognita of the Stone House attic.

On her next summer visit to Treetops, my mother moved out of Hemlock—the little Goldilocks cottage under the trees—and into the Stone House. She bought furniture to replace the missing pieces. She had the chairs and sofa reupholstered, brought a huge oriental carpet from Ossining for the living room floor, and installed an antique wood-burning stove in the kitchen. The rest of the house stayed untouched, like a country shrine to Polly's chic city taste. The heavy silk curtains gathered dust and their knotted drawstrings tangled. My mother stayed there each summer, but many of my cousins avoided it. "I wouldn't want to stay in the Stone House," my cousin Dr. Robert Mellors, Jane's son, said. "It's like a museum." In spite of my mother's changes, the air in and around the Stone House remains heavily charged with the past.

Upstairs in Polly's bedroom are more silk curtains, a flowered Fortuny bedspread, now badly torn, and the curlicued wrought iron standing lamps with painted shades that Winter had made for all the Treetops cottages. Under the bedroom window sits a mauve, bolstered chaise-longue, a piece of furniture that still speaks of women of leisure lounging through long, hot afternoons while they read novels and eat chocolate creams—or doze off the effect of too many sherries at lunch.

Downstairs, off the living room, Winter's study is dominated by the large, lifelike drawing of him on the wall opposite the windows, the light blocked now by rhododendron bushes. This room smells of inky papers and books, and Winter's stationery is still neatly piled in one drawer. Outside, Polly's lily pond is overgrown with spiky juniper, her cutting garden is a dwarf forest of spindly second-growth saplings, but on the stairs at the Stone House, you can still almost hear her telling Winter that, if he wants to communicate with her, he can reach her through Thomas Cook.

The real ghost at Treetops is the ghost of Peter Weesul. When he died in 1967, he had been working the land of that hillside every day, summer and winter, for almost fifty years. On cold nights when I slept at the Stone House after 1975, I would wake up at dawn every morning to hear Peter open the heavy front door downstairs and walk down the echoing frame staircase to the big cellar to bring up fresh logs for the huge fireplace that dominates the Stone House living room. There would be the unlatching and creaking sounds as the big door opened, a moment of silence as he crossed the kitchen linoleum floor in the high-top sneakers he always wore, and then the booming noise of his descent. Sometimes I heard him leave, too, although he never went as far as the living room, where I could have seen him, if I could have seen him, by peeking down over the balcony.

When I stayed in the Stone House during the winter, the sounds of Peter coming and going from the cellar, where the furnace had to be stoked, were louder and more regular. As I lay in Polly's bed, I could hear him down there pulling logs off the woodpile, pulling open the iron door of the furnace, and shoving the logs in above the smoking bed of coals. I would sometimes catch a whiff of his woodsy, sweaty smell, left behind in the kitchen or on the cellar stairs.

Sometimes on a summer day, looking up the steep pitch of dirt road toward the Stone House from the bend where Peter Weesul's old farmhouse still stands—converted into condominium apartments—even now, in the shadows of the pines as they shift in the breeze, I'll see old Peter riding the high bench at the front of his cart with Horse Weesul in front of him, trudging up to work in the gardens of the past.

⬧

Treetops in the years after Winter died in 1959 was a pretty jolly place. Although Buff took over, doing the accounts, hiring the help, planning the meals, and equaling her father's arbitrary favoritism in assigning visitors to cottages, she could not equal his frightening authority. When Aunt Buff was killed in 1972, it seemed to signal the end of a long line of Treetops disciplinarians. There was a what-the-hell atmosphere, a let-it-all-go-to-rack-and-ruin mood. The old rules were broken. No one dressed for dinner or showed up on time for lunch. Vegetables were bought instead of picked. There was beer in the refrigerator and a bottle of whiskey in the cupboard under the shelves of willowware china where the flatware had been. One of my cousins used Winter's laboratory in the garage to brew moonshine from windfall apples, and every now and then we'd walk down the steep incline to the Stone House to have a few too many drinks with Polly or the Whitney aunts and uncles who sometimes stayed there at her invitation.

As Peter Weesul weakened, the place began to crumble. Gardens went to seed and their fences sagged and fell. Weeds grew everywhere and the roofs began to leak. For decades, Treetops had been a place where everything was taken care of. It was that Shangri-la in all our dreams where we are free to play and work, come and go, while someone else is responsible for fixing the plumbing and doing the repairs and paying utility bills.

Treetops had in fact required constant upkeep. Now the New Hampshire climate had its way. Shingles blew off, windows shattered. Squirrels came down the chimney and chewed through doors and sashes trying to escape. Bats nested in the eaves, hornets built their nests on exposed rafters, porcupines and woodchucks chewed holes in the foundations.

After Peter's death, my mother and her brothers and sisters— who were then in their fifties—acted like children who had been let loose in their parents' house while their parents were away. There was a succession of disastrous hired hands. One totaled the pickup truck and another disappeared with all the guns and a bottle of whiskey. Another, who had spent years in the merchant marine, adorned almost everything on the place with nautical motifs. A life preserver painted with the legend "S.S. Treetops" decorated the side of the boat house.

The younger generation took advantage of the relaxing of the guard. An ancient convertible car and an old rattletrap truck were used to ferry us back and forth between Treetops and the state liquor store in Bristol. At night we headed for the Country Belle, a ramshackle barn out on the main road where blasting rock music attracted hordes of townies on Saturday nights.

There were plenty of pranks and mischief. My brother Ben and my cousin Bill Winternitz, who had been deported from Nantucket Island for stealing signs, brought their technique and their college boy zeal for theft to Treetops. We swam in the lake late at night and then paddled the canoe by moonlight stealthily to other people's docks, where we partied until the sounds of shouts and sirens interrupted our revels and drove us back into the canoe for the silent trip home. The year-round neighbors were horrified. The Blakes, who had the beach adjoining our beach, put up a huge No Trespassing sign on their dock, facing our boat house. When my cousin Paul Winternitz, who wore his hair in a ponytail, went skinny-dipping one evening, Mrs. Blake called the police. They arrived and escorted him to the Bristol jail with all the good manners the police reserved for unidentified vagrant hippies. After a telephone call from his father, he was quickly released. We all thought this was very funny.

My mother often told me how her father, in the last years of his life, had scrimped and saved to put together a trust fund for Treetops, so that his children and their children would be able to continue to maintain it. I didn't listen. We were all children at Treetops. Even our parents were children.

183

Without Winter and Polly to assign them to cottages, the four children who regularly visited Treetops settled into the one that suited them. Buff took charge of Balsam, the cottage at the edge of the woods where a narrow path leads across the pine needles and over a three-board bridge to the more rustic Bushes. Balsam is the most houselike cottage, with a stone fireplace and French doors that open from the living room to a long porch outside. For a while, my mother stayed in Hemlock, the smallest, darkest cottage. Bill adopted Pine, Grandpa and Grandma Watson's cottage, with the big double bed in the main room (in Grandma Watson's time it was a Murphy bed built by Grandpa, which folded up against the wall during the day). When Tom and Betty went to Treetops, they usually stayed, as they had in Winter's time, in Spruce, the former servants' quarters over the garage.

During the late sixties and early seventies, Treetops was often empty. Usually no one showed up until August, and everyone left after Labor Day. New Hampshire itself seemed like a family secret. The commuters who have made it one of the fastest growing states in the Union hadn't discovered how close it is to Boston. In those days when vacations meant the beach, people paid inflated prices for tiny pieces of land near the ocean while beautiful Victorian houses in mostly landlocked New Hampshire disintegrated because no one wanted them.

For years, the cottages and outbuildings of Treetops, Peter Weesul and Pete Charron's farmhouses, and two other small houses owned by Dr. Osgood and Dr. Blake further up the hill were the only structures on the road except for a tar paper shack in the woods which was the summer home of the local hermit. When Dr. Osgood died, his place was abandoned. The barn roof collapsed on his old car, and weeds and scrub grew up in front of the house, cutting off the lake view and creating one of the richest blueberry patches in the state. Pete Charron's barn caved in, and Peter Weesul's farmhouse after he died looked like something out of a Walker Evans Depression photograph. The hill and the surrounding countryside had all the marks of rural poverty, from the age-wizened, overweight bodies of the natives, whose diet was based on the New England staples of bread and fudge, to the For Sale signs that appeared in the summer on everything from livestock to real estate.

❧

In the 1980s, Treetops grew up. My aunts and uncles, as they reached old age, have taken charge of the place at last. The rest of the family seems belatedly to have realized that the hillside is a treasure, and that treasure should be protected. In 1983, my Uncle Bill organized a Winternitz family partnership, and all the partners—Bill, Tom, my mother, Jane, and Elizabeth's two children—entered into an agreement that protects both the property and Winter's intent. No partner can sell or rent their shares. If a partner dies and the shares come on the market, they must be offered first to the partnership. No interest in the partnership is transferable—even to husbands or wives.

"It is to be the primary . . . purpose of this Agreement to insure that the real estate lying and being in Grafton County, State of New Hampshire and now held by the partners individually . . . is maintained and kept up for the benefit of the partners and their families, even if in doing so Partnership income is completely exhausted," the agreement states.

As managing partner, Uncle Bill has instituted annual as-

sessments for all of us who use Treetops, to augment the existing trust fund left by Winter. The once leaky, sagging cottages
have been shored up and painted, there are new appliances in
Apple and a washer-dryer in the laundry, and the encroaching
New Hampshire wilderness has been beaten back by lawn
mowers and farm equipment.

There is also new activity at the Stone House. Uncle Tom's
wife, Aunt Betty, has moved in and "modernized" it with an oil
burner and new rules which no one observes. The house feels
cleaner, smaller, and more ordinary. It no longer smells of wood
smoke and rotting silk and old books, the ghosts of cigarettes
and spilled martinis and lavender. The walls have been painted
and repapered, the attic cleaned out, the chimney fortified
against bats and squirrels, a push-button phone installed, and
a new waterline run in from the wells up the hill. The sounds of
Peter Weesul are gone.

Instead of the caretaker misfits and local boys who replaced
Peter Weesul in the carefree sixties, Treetops now has a full-
time, bona fide caretaker, who looks more like the Squire of
Treetops than do any of its actual owners. A graceful New
Hampshire aristocrat, Sherburn Ramsay, Jr., is a retired schoolteacher with the manners and presence of authority. He's a
handsome man with lots of white hair, a ruddy face, and a
burly body clothed with unconscious style in work pants, red
suspenders, and a plaid flannel shirt. He wears a cap, taking it
off to wipe his brow with a red bandanna. He drives a pickup.
At noontime he consults a big gold watch with the Liberty Bell
embossed on its cover, pulling it from his pocket and snapping
it open in one gesture. If Uncle Bill hadn't hired him, Ralph
Lauren probably would have.

If Treetops has come alive again, Sherb Ramsay has been the attending physician. He's the one person who's always there, and he watches with amusement as different branches of the family come and go. Invited correctly, Sherb will come sit in the kitchen of Apple or the living room of the Stone House, drink a cup of coffee or a beer, and chat about the weather, taxes, and the future of Grafton County real estate. He has a way of making each of us feel that we're his favorite member of the family. He tells the little girls how pretty they are and takes the boys for rides on his tractor.

On the third weekend in August, we usually drive down Peaked Hill and up Dick Brown's road to the Bridgewater Grange Hall for a local celebration called Old Home Day. Bridgewater was densely settled in the 1830s and 1840s. The Civil War and the movement of the textile industry from New England to the South turned it into a ghost town. These days some of the old houses have been reclaimed by summer people—but the town still has more empty cellar holes than houses. High on Bridgewater Mountain at a steep junction of dirt roads, the Grange Hall is almost inaccessible much of the year. In August, Bridgewater families and neighbors get together for a communal baked bean lunch, a tour of the graveyard and the cellar holes, a square dance, and a service in the old Grange Hall.

The square dance is like something out of *Ethan Frome*. A crippled caller sings out the steps as local people in their dancing clothes—the men in jeans, the women in faded calico—do the Grand Promenade. Crowds of children giggle in the corners, and babies sleep on stacks of sweaters and old quilts next to the podium at the front of the room. Old Home Day is a remembrance of the people who settled Bridgewater two hundred years ago, eking out a grim living from the rocky soil way up here a million miles from anywhere.

In the morning we all troop into the Grange Hall for a service. Our voices echo in the wooden rafters of the small frame building, a building constructed out of hope as the center of a town that was already dying. "A mighty fortress is our God," we sing, huddled together over shared hymnals, "a bulwark never failing." Our frail, hopeful voices carry out through the open doors and windows of the hall. At the end of our rustic wooden pew, my cousin Frank, a long way from his cathedral in Chicago, rests his hand on one of his daughters' shoulders. His wife Phoebe holds their hymnal, but she looks up as she sings Martin Luther's words. "Our helper He amid the flood, of mortal ills prevailing."

We stand, a few of us together in what is still a crossroads in the wilderness, singing about the past and what we look to as the future, as generations before us stood here and sang. It's a sunny day and the song travels uphill from the Grange Hall across the high meadows and over the apple orchards and through the birch trees at the edge of the forest until it finally fades away, somewhere deep in the golden woods where the ruins of stone walls built by the earliest Bridgewater farmers crumble down into moss and ferns and pine needles. In this part of New Hampshire, nature rules. Our fragile voices lift on the mountain wind, fade, and quickly disappear into the summer air.

EIGHTEEN

IT'S TEN O'CLOCK on the morning of June 12, 1988. My brother
Ben and I are sitting on a wooden bench in a windowless room
in the federal courthouse of the Southern District Court in
White Plains. Judge Gerard L. Goettel leans forward from the
bench toward the stenographer, who sits with her fingers tap-
ping automatically on one of the brown chairs that are part of
the soulless beige and brown decoration scheme. My mother is
on the stand.

"Do you, Mary Winternitz Cheever, solemnly swear . . . ?"

My mother raises her right hand to take the oath. I notice that
she still wears her wedding ring. Although she's seventy years
old, she moves like a young woman. This morning she's
dressed in a white sweater and a neat tan poplin skirt. Most of
my mother's women friends are alone. Many spend their days
visiting, gardening, and waiting for their lives to end. Instead,
she's the central figure in this courtroom drama. She swears to
tell the truth, the whole truth, and nothing but the truth.

"On the afternoon of December 12th, 1987, did you spend more than an hour with the defendant's representative?" asks Academy Chicago's lawyer, a tall man in an ill-fitting suit who appears to think he's a character in "L.A. Law." His tone is accusatory, but my mother is not easily shaken.

"I didn't want to be rude to the young man," she explains, ignoring the lawyer and turning to speak to the judge. "I had the experience, then, which I did not recognize, . . . that my civility, courtesy, was mistaken for complaisance."

In the summer of 1987, my mother signed a two-page contract with Academy Chicago, a small publishing house owned and operated by Jordan and Anita Miller. The contract specified that my mother was the so-called author of their proposed book of uncollected short stories by John Cheever and that the book would be published at a mutually agreeable date. It was accompanied by a letter from the publisher's representative, Franklin Dennis, dismissing the contract itself as a formality and stating that my mother would have, of course, control over the contents of the book. Unfortunately, the contract was fatally vague on the subject of how many, and exactly which, "uncollected short stories by John Cheever" my mother was giving permission to publish. Her understanding, based on her conversations with the gentlemanly Jordan Miller, was that they planned a small book of five to seven stories, but this understanding was not spelled out.

Judge Goettel leans forward and smiles. He's a man about my mother's age with white hair and a round face. They seem to come from the same genteel world. He will not betray her assumptions. Above his head the clock ticks, and behind us reporters scribble notes. The Millers and their family sit in the benches with blank faces.

"Didn't you know where all the stories were?" asks the lawyer.

"Some of them were in magazines that have been out of print for a long time."

Judge Goettel interrupts the questioning of my mother. "A number of these stories were written before you ever met your husband?" he asks. My mother leans toward him and smiles at the nice man behind the bench. At last, her demeanor suggests, an intelligent question.

"Oh, long before," she says. "When he was a boy of eighteen." In her voice there is pride at my father's achievement.

"Did he keep a running file?" the judge wants to know.

"He kept no files, no correspondence, no letters, nothing." My mother and the judge are chatting away like old friends while Academy Chicago's lawyer fumes and paces in front of the courtroom.

"Not very businesslike," clucks Judge Goettel.

"Not at all," my mother agrees.

"Like most authors," says the judge.

"That's right," my mother smiles at the bench again.

"Now, Mrs. Cheever!" the lawyer interrupts angrily. "You said . . . that you considered it part of Mr. Dennis' job . . . to ascertain the circumstances under which the various stories were written." My mother starts and turns as if surprised that this maniac is allowed to involve himself in her nice talk with the judge.

"I believe I said that I imagined that might be some of the

function of an editor," she says. "I didn't realize that Mr. Dennis is less than competent."

"And just how did you expect Mr. Dennis to go about doing that?"

"When I was a teacher, I taught something called the research paper." My mother turns and directs her explanation to the judge. Is it all right to answer? she seems to be asking. He nods his approval. "And I learned all the sources that there are for locating the works of any particular author." Now she turns on the lawyer indignantly. "If [Mr. Dennis] had been a student of mine, I would have given him perhaps a C-plus for effort. . . . The research was incomplete, the product was sloppy, and he had no thesis whatever, no idea how to arrange or select these stories, *no thesis whatever.*"

Judge Goettel showed his sympathy for my mother when he wrote his decision. He had no more use than she did for a literary promoter like Franklin Dennis or publishers like Jordan Miller and his wife. Although he found for her in federal court, putting a restraining order on publication of the book (*and concluding that my mother had not transferred her copyrights*), he declined to decide whether or not the contract itself was valid.

As a result, in the fall of 1988, we went to trial again, in the Illinois State Court in Chicago before Judge Roger Kiley. Judge Kiley also found for my mother, writing that, although she owed Academy Chicago a book of "uncollected stories of John Cheever," the book should be made up of stories chosen, edited, and selected by her. We submitted a book of fifteen stories and an introduction to Academy Chicago. Judge Kiley ruled specifically that our submitted book satisfied our obligations under the contract my mother had signed. Academy Chicago is appealing this decision, although the Illinois Appeals Court rejected their first appeal last July.

Three years after my mother signed the original contract, she is still embroiled in lawsuits with Academy Chicago, and her debt in legal fees is an astronomical $700,000 plus. This is the way she has spent part of the last years of her life, years when she might have been expected to relax and take advantage of the lessening responsibilities that sometimes come with age. Instead she has gone to war to protect her part of the inheritance left by my father's talent. It was a talent that caused her pain, but it was also a talent she admired and respected. Like her mother and her grandmother, she was married to an extraordinary man. Like the women of her generation, she focused her energy on the development of her husband's gifts rather than on discovering her own. She is willing to fight for my father as fiercely as she used to fight with him.

NINETEEN

In 1957 MY family returned from a year of living in Italy. We brought back Iole Felici, a country woman who had been hired as a housekeeper and a nurse for my brother Fred, who was born in Rome. Iole had very strong ideas about everything, from the raising of children to the way the gentry should behave, and her manner in the family settled into a benevolent scolding. Eventually Fred grew up and Iole moved on, marrying the gardener on the Vanderlip estate and, when the gardener died, going to work for a wealthy lawyer in Ossining. Iole had always scolded our family for our disdain for physical comforts. My parents didn't dress well enough, she said. The house wasn't even decorated, or decorated as if it was a monastery.

In her new employer and his house, sumptuously decorated by his late wife in pinks and greens, with layers of drapes and shelves of Meissen figurines, Iole at last found her ideal of how the American upper class should live. When he was away, Iole would take Fred—by then a student in law school—over to his house and demonstrate how proper people lived. "See!" she would exclaim, opening closets filled with shoes, all carefully matched and polished—unlike the heap of old shoes in my father's closet—"this is how a man should live!" She was entranced by the many sets of china in silver slip covers and the abundance of furniture and the way his wardrobe was organized into neckties and matching shirts which went so nicely with his cashmere suits.

Because of Iole, Herbert and the way he lived became a family joke. As a result, we all laughed—including my mother—when he guided his Oldsmobile down the narrow driveway a few months after my father died to come pay court to the widow Cheever.

Herbert was a courtly, old-fashioned gentleman who liked to pick my mother up in his car—he always walked around it to hold the door open for her—and take her to Maison Lafitte, the local posh restaurant, an elaborately French establishment in an old mansion with a view of the Hudson. My mother laughed with us about Herbert's taste in clothes and his clumsy passes, and Herbert's country club set friends, until one day my mother called me up and told me that Iole had found her in bed with Herbert when she came into his bedroom in the morning. For Iole, who had been intensely loyal to my father in all his difficulties with my mother, but who, after all, had held Herbert up to us as the ideal man, it must have been a disconcerting moment.

Herbert and my mother settled into an arrangement which seemed to work well. They maintained separate family lives, and they each lived on in the house which was—in both cases—a sort of shrine to their dead spouse. Although the

houses were only a few miles apart from each other in Ossining, Herbert's house with its ornamentation and ostentatious
comfort, was light-years away from my mother's house with its
minimal decoration, hard antique chairs, and worn oriental
rugs. My mother had lived for years with a man with intense
feelings about her and an acid, sarcastic way of expressing
them. Herbert's distance was a relief.

Herbert was a trim, handsome old man with blue eyes, who
often told us about how he had seen President Roosevelt's
inauguration from the branches of a tree where he had climbed
to get a better view. His brother, Joe, was a prizefighter who,
Herbert said, had thrown the 1924 Olympics on a point of
honor. Herbert had been a lawyer for Paramount and he liked to
talk about the famous people he had known and seen in a
world which seemed indescribably ancient and long ago. He
was a passionate collector of Presidential signatures.

As his friendship with my mother grew, I used to urge my
brother Ben, in his role as the oldest Cheever male, to take Herb
out to lunch and ask what his intentions were toward our
mother. The farthest Herb and my mother got in this direction
was one formal dinner at which my husband and I were offi-
cially introduced to Herb and his family. It was a bizarre
evening—beginning with Iole greeting us at the door and ex-
claiming in intimate terms about my appearance as if I was still
twelve years old. I sat in Herb's pink and green living room, as
foreign to our neighboring house as if they were from different
planets, and wondered if my mother would marry him.

It was really clear, though, that marriage was impossible.

One of them would have had to give up the past in the form of their house and move in with the other's past. They were too old, and too set to start over. Also, Herbert was rich and his family lived in fear that he would marry my mother and split the inheritance they were counting on.

But in the summer of 1985, three years after he first came to call on my mother, Herbert got sick and was operated on for pancreatic cancer at New York University Hospital. Once again, my mother lived through the long death of someone she cared about. She didn't talk about it. We didn't talk about it.

Herbert's funeral service was at Frank Campbell on Madison Avenue. My mother sat near the back as the rabbi, who hadn't spoken personally to Herbert in years, talked about his passionate love for his dead wife, Josephine. My mother didn't say anything about it afterward. Sometimes she acts as if there's no place in the world for her. The other day she told me that she didn't have much hope about having company in her old age.

"But you got along with Herbert," I said. "That could happen again."

"Oh Herbert," she said with a snort. "That was just sex."

TWENTY

TREETOPS WAS BUILT with profits from the invention of the telephone, but the telephone system there is about as efficient as two tin cans tied together with a waxed string. There is one number for two telephones—at the top of the hill in Apple and at the bottom of the hill in the Stone House. When someone in the Stone House picks up a call for someone in one of the cottages or vice versa, they must resort to the only means of communication between the two houses besides a shout—a 1912 crank telephone with a separate receiver on a hook and a buttercup mouthpiece mounted on a wooden plaque. The bell for this picturesque apparatus is an iron crank, and by energetic, rapid cranking it is sometimes possible to produce a rusty ringing at the other end of the line. Like a lot of things at Treetops, it belongs more to the past than to the present.

As New Hampshire has changed, Treetops has become more and more an isolated outpost where things are done the old way. The narrow road at the bottom of the hill which runs between the road and the lake is now a straightaway on a wide highway where logging and freight trucks practice getting their speed up, playing chicken with passing cars. There are a dozen new houses on Peaked Hill, most of them split-level ranch houses put up by builders on speculation and bought by commuting families who tear up and down the widened road on their way to and from their jobs. For years we knew everyone who lived on Peaked Hill, and the road was like a private driveway; now drivers pass each other at the entrance to Treetops without even a friendly wave.

There have been two fires at Treetops—the fire that destroyed Balsam and a second fire on June 19, 1982, the day after my father died in the upstairs bedroom of my parents' house in Ossining. Someone set fire to one of the old chicken coops. Although there had been no chickens since my grandfather died, the coop was intact—a shrine to the chickens of the past— and its mixture of old sawdust, wooden nests and ladders, and dried-out boards went up like kindling, igniting a fast-burning blaze that sent a column of smoke into the sky above Peaked Hill. Sparks and flames flew toward the woods, which were fortunately damp from spring rain, and settled on the small shed where Peter Weesul had kept some of his gardening tools. By the time the Bristol Fire Department got there and hitched up their hoses to the well, the chicken house was burned to the ground and the shed a sagging teepee of charred timbers.

A few nights later, the local police caught a vagrant who they said was the arsonist. He had stolen blankets and clothing from nearby Camp Tomahawk, and he had set fire to some abandoned tourist cabins down on Route 3A near the Pasquaney Inn.

By the time I drove up to Treetops at the end of June, the man had been shipped north to the state prison. But he had escaped from the police before they were able to incarcerate him, and he had been seen back in the neighborhood of Camp Tomahawk down by the lake.

Alone in the Stone House, I would look out the lighted windows into the darkening woods as night fell and wonder if there was a man out there who would be looking back as soon as the light faded and I couldn't see anything else beyond my reflection in the glass. I thought of the Frost poem, written nearby on Bridgewater Mountain when Frost spent summers there, about being trapped in a New Hampshire house during a winter storm. "I count our strength." More than ever I was alert to the savage force of nature always waiting to be released in the New Hampshire wilderness. The night quiet, the absolute stillness at twilight as the sun sank behind Cardigan Mountain, sounded like the silence of an animal about to spring.

My Uncle Bill arrived and moved into Pine, the large cottage up the hill on the other side of Winter's old laboratory. I took some comfort from thinking that a scream at the Stone House would probably be heard up there. I knew that it would be impossible for him to hear the old-fashioned jangle of the hand-cranked telephone bell, even if I could get it to work.

But soon Treetops was crowded again. My mother came, and some cousins, and the days faded into the clear hot mountain days and cold starry nights of every other Treetops summer. Each summer there has a name: 1982 was the summer the chicken coops burned down, 1971 was the summer I had my last birthday there, 1969 was the summer the flood washed out the road, 1959 was Winter's last summer, 1948 was the summer the pig fell into the well. They all form a continuum stretching back into the past when my parents were children and forward into my children's lives, a continuum of family ties and feuds and swimming in the transparent green water of the lake and sleeping under the fragrant pinewood roofs of the cottages, and remembering the past.

My mother is seventy-two years old this year. Once she was a grandchild at Treetops, now she is a grandmother. She still goes up there every summer, loading clothes and furniture and odds and ends and the dog into her station wagon and driving nonstop up Route 84 to Hartford and then up to Sturbridge across the Massachusetts state line and over to Route 93 and up into New Hampshire.

She gets there in the late afternoon, stops at the lake to go for a swim, and then moves into Hemlock, the cottage tucked into the land below the oval lawn. As the day ends she walks across the lawn to the kitchen in Apple, has a whiskey with whomever else is there, and sits down to dinner at the long table on the porch.

I can see her there in my imagination more clearly than anywhere else, passing the corn or the peas as the light fades over the orchard and moths bang against the screens, and the evening star appears above the fires of sunset behind the mountains. Wherever she is, she'll always be there with the rest of them, the living and the dead, leaning over the table her grandfather built, sitting in her father's big wicker chair, watching as darkness falls softly over the view her mother fell in love with so many years ago.

NOTE

IN MANY WAYS this book is a collective act of memory. It's family history pieced together from casual stories, letters, and the remembered days and nights of those who were part of it. My mother, especially, spent hours talking with me about her family, elucidating and clarifying incidents I vaguely recalled and filling in the gaps. Her brothers, my Uncles Tom and Bill Winternitz, were also willing to answer my questions and talk freely about the past and their family. Stephen Whitney wrote me a long letter about his days at Treetops and Janie Whitney Hotchkiss and her family were hospitable, cooperative and witty. My own brothers, Benjamin and Federico, contributed not only their own recollections of our days at Treetops, but their thoughts about my mother, her childhood, and my parents, and tried to help unravel the narrative and ethical tangles of our past together. A great deal of the book is based on the collection of my grandfather's papers which he left to his son, my Uncle Bill, and which Bill generously left at Yale.

The original idea for the book came from conversations with my husband, Warren Hinckle, and my agent, Andrew Wylie, both men who know how to push ideas to the limit. My editor, Deb Futter, helped me put the ideas into words. I'm indebted to many friends and colleagues who, directly or without knowing it, have helped me struggle through the enervating and exhilarating process of writing a book. Most of all I have to thank my children, Warren IV and Sarah. They are what I live for.